T0158062

How
To
Become

TRAPPED *to* SUCCEED™

A Neuro **P**sych **S**cience **G**uide on the **P**sychology of **S**uccess.

A New Branch

Of

Success Psychology

Eric F. Prince

M.A.Ed./M.S.A.P/PhD: Candidate Clinical Psychology – Forensic Psychology

Book Interior by Eric F. Prince

Author Photos by Marc Hauser Photography

Order this book online at www.trafford.com
or email orders@trafford.com

Most Trafford titles are also available at major online book retailers.

Scripture quotations marked KJV are from the Holy Bible, King James Version
(Authorized Version). First published in 1611. Quoted from the KJV Classic
Reference Bible, Copyright © 1983 by The Zondervan Corporation.

Print information available on the last page.

ISBN: 978-1-4907-8816-6 (sc)
ISBN: 978-1-4907-8815-9 (hc)
ISBN: 978-1-4907-8818-0 (e)

Library of Congress Control Number: 2018939958

Trafford rev. 05/14/2020

 www.trafford.com

North America & international
toll-free: 1 888 232 4444 (USA & Canada)
fax: 812 355 4082

ERIC FRANKLIN PRINCE

Graduated, or is a current student, or member of the
the following organizations and academic institutions:
The United States Coast Guard Auxiliary Unit: FSO-DV and
NACO 3 Star Award Recipient. To Commanders Keith Destree
Jeff Bailey from the International Port of Chicago,
and Ed Samson from Mission Bay San Diego: God Speed!
The Chicago Police Academy
Recipient of the Physical Fitness Merit Award in his graduating Class
Current M.S.A.P holder and PhD Candidate of
Clinical Psychology at Walden University where the clinical
psychology program is based on the scholar, scientist-practitioner
model. M.A.Ed holder and alumni of Azusa Pacific University
with a BA in Human Development.
ASAJ/AA: Social and Behavioral Studies Riverside Community College -
AA. Liberal Arts: Social and Behavioral Studies San Bernardino Valley
College – Phillips College of Chicago AA: Travel Tourism –
Pi Lambda Theta Honor Society – Golden Key Honor Society –
Psi Chi Honor Society – Alpha Phi Sigma Honor Society/Walden
University Phi Nu Chapter – Academy of Criminal Justice
Sciences and the American Criminal Justice Association:
Lambda Alpha Epsilon - Salute Honor Society – Student Veterans

Affairs Association – National Honor Society of Human
Services – National Society of Leadership and Success – Full Bright
Association – American Psychological Association's Emerging
Leadership Academy - National Institute of Mental
Health (NIH) Office of Extramural
Human Subjects Research (HSR) – CITI Program
The Chicago Board of Education as a licensed educator
Illinois American Psychological Association - American Psychological
Association of Graduate Students - The American Psychological
Federal Action Network which deals with legislative issues that
impact human welfare and the profession of psychology on Capitol
Hill. Current Screen Actors Guild (SAG) member and current DD
Theology student at Beyth-'El Temple and Private College under
the tutelage of Pastor/Educator Chief Apostle Y. B. Amen, Ph.D.

To my beloved family ¥isra'el, you have the power to bless the world, so bless them. Never give up on your visions or your dreams; for they are the very essence of what makes you the salt of the earth!

For without Christ, there is no true success! Therefore, I thank Christ for giving me the power to become trapped to succeed. For in You, Christ, the possibilities are endless!

To the little children who will get their hands on this book, and you will. You will know that I am talking about you. Do not doubt yourself. Believe in yourself with all your heart. You can and will do great things in life! You are growing, developing, and maturing rapidly. Do not waste your time. Live, laugh, learn, grow, and know that you are special, no matter what you may be going through. The creator, God Almighty, through Christ, is your very present help during troubling times.

Lastly, this book is dedicated to those who never give up on their dreams and to those who have dreams but may not necessarily know how to go about accomplishing them.

I would rather have written one book in a lifetime, than started many and finished none.

This quote was inspired by all those who told me that they have started many books but have never finished and/or published any of them.

The time is now!

Just do it!

CONTENTS

A very special thank-you to Christ, my Lord and Savior; my mother; my pastor, father, and friend, Chief Apostle Y. B. Amen, PhD; Ame Apostle Sarah Amen; Winesha Whitehead (Nesha). I thank you all for being there for me and my family, especially when things got rough. Know that 'til the end of time, you will always be appreciated. For it is the spirit by which one serves mankind in their darkest hours that displays the true essence of one's nature.

Trapped To Succeed™

INTRODUCTION

What does it mean to be trapped to succeed? Does the concept of being trapped to succeed actually exist? If so, how does one become trapped to succeed? These are some of the questions I asked myself before I found out that by God's power, and that of constant growth and development through human evolution, I could become trapped to succeed, which could occur during my lifetime.

I discovered that myself and others of the human race could actually become trapped to succeed. It does not matter whether you are rich or poor, nor what race or background that an individual is associated with or comes from, but rather, the mind, heart, soul, and spirit of the person who applies himself or herself to the goal that he or she seeks. There are many levels of seeking, learning, and growing.

The key factor is what level will you be on and to what degree will you submerge yourself in knowledge that will take you further for a better future.

As you embark upon this journey with me, into the realm of being trapped to succeed, we will walk through spiritual heights, explore wide spectrums of data that come from empirical findings, retrospective analysis, phenomenological events that explore critical data from case studies that can actually cause one to become successful every time they start out to accomplish a goal, dream, or aspiration—if they will apply this knowledge to their lives! You will learn what an effective strategy is and how to utilize an effective strategy in your life and on your level. You will learn how to maintain your confidence and how to focus on your goals to reach them hands down!

You will learn how to overcome obstacles that truthfully come to destroy you! People say trials come to make you strong, but they don't—trials come to destroy, but one gets stronger by overcoming the obstacles and learning how to deal with future problems. If one cannot deal successfully with problems, that person will never become successful, and if they should so happen to do so, it will not last. Problems will always be around; it's how we as human beings deal with them that makes us strong and enables us to become a success!

So come and take this walk with me, and together, let's begin this journey, which we will navigate and conquer our dreams by ways of strategic methods, making our dreams no longer aspirations but positive realities in the world in which we live!

I decided to not only write a book, but also build a resource that is based on empirical evidence that has been substantiated with peer-reviewed journal articles and evidence-based practices that would open people's eyes and minds in a very real way to what it means to be successful, along with the struggles that one will face when seeking to obtain success. I hope that this will be the case with this book. I have built something that, I think, is worth looking into, and I hope society, on a global scale, will come and partake in my endeavor to help them become trapped to succeed.

Know again, this is not the typical book that I have written; it is not the traditional type of self-help book but rather, to some degree, a blueprint that is carefully woven into a manuscript type of document that will assist societal members at large in being successful in a way that is by no means ordinary. It is very possible that this document is extraordinary in nature because of its deep, complex concepts, which are synthesized with new insights that are both spiritual and scientific in nature.

It was critical to figure out a way to incorporate psychotherapy, talk therapy, cognitive-based therapy into this book and to do it in a way that a great deal of people would receive it without being bored to death while reading. It should also be known that the goal of psychology is to make people better by opening their understanding and by modifying their behaviors for better life spans.

Again, this is my way of giving back to society, through talk therapy in relationship to matters of overcoming obstacles and becoming successful. This book is also less expensive than therapy sessions and can assist them in today's economy as described by the article in Annals of the American Psychotherapy/Association (2010). It is important to note that this book is not meant to replace talk therapy but to be a positive force in the field of psychology, which will assist people who do read books for the sake of time management and/or financial budgeting while encouraging them to seek talk therapy once they can afford it.

Furthermore, it is my desire that those who read this book will study it while taking critical notes. Doing so, will provide a person with higher levels of gaining more insight into the therapeutic concepts that are listed in this book which will show them how to go about being successful in today's economy. Talk therapy can be highly effective for various situations, although many people feel vulnerable as discussed in an article written in the Annals of the American Psychotherapy/ Association, 2010.

After all, this is a new era we are living in, and things are rapidly changing, which is why there are more people reading self-help books, and let me say there are many great authors out there!

Many people are out of work and need assistance from various sources. This book is constructed to be one of those sources. People are thinking deeper and more innovative than ever before. The world as we know it is changing, and if we as the human race fail to keep up with the intelligent movement, we will be left behind. We as human beings must be smarter, sharper, and a lot tougher. It's just the way it is now. We have to micromanage ourselves, be more organized, and be more meticulous in our planning and in the execution of those plans. It's your time to go back to the drawing board. It's time to go deeper in the way you are thinking so that you can go further than ever before!

Message from the Author

As you read this book, I want you to remember that no matter how many left and right hooks life throws you, if you don't give up on yourself, you can and will overcome. Life is full of twists and turns and many other obstacles and elements that will make you feel like giving up, and you may feel that those problems are only happening to you, that you are the only one with problems in the world. This couldn't be further from the truth. We all have our struggles, problems, trials, tribulations, and other negative situations that arise in our lives, but you must remember, only the strong shall survive!

Believe me when I tell you, you are not the only one facing hardships. Many people go through various problems in life on a day-to-day basis. You'll never know what the next person is going through, so don't think you're the only one going through the storm. Rather, be more concerned about making it through the storm and coming out victorious on the other end.

Know that you will survive if you fight to succeed. I constantly remind myself to adapt to situations around me so that I will not be destroyed. If you do not learn how to adapt to a changing environment, you will not overcome and be successful. Human beings live in a world where things constantly change, sometimes for the worse and sometimes for the better.

The psychological component is, therefore, this: Can you change with an ever-changing world without folding and/or giving up under pressure? If you can, this is called resilience! (Brew & Kottler, 2008; Ivey, Ivey, & Zalaquett, 2013) Can you overcome your own negative emotions and be resilient where you can bounce back and get back in the fight to win? Yes, you can! But it's up to you. We are all social beings that have to interact with others; we must seek to understand our core motives and how we function best in society. (Fiske, 2014) It's all about learning how to deal with the situations that are at hand without succumbing to the pressures of life.

Remember, without failure, there can be no success. Don't be afraid to fail sometimes. Some of the world's greatest people failed first and then succeeded down the road. A good case study to read is the story of the world's greatest basketball player. His name is Michael Jordan.

Learn how to be a warrior and stand up for your goals, dreams, and visions. "For without a vision, the people perish" (KJV). Remember no positive dream is unattainable if you put your mind to it. Christ said, "Let this mind be in you, which is in Christ" (KJV). Challenges are a part of everyday life. Some obstacles may seem gigantic, but they can be overcome with a little patience, time, dedication, and perseverance that will ultimately see you through. There is no obstacle too big to be cast down if your put God first. If no one else has done what you are trying to do, lead the way! If others have trail-blazed, you follow the paths that they have left for you.

Remember, if you don't have dreams, they cannot come true— dream a little! Know where you want to go in life. Without the pursuit of obtaining goals, there will be no accomplishments, so set your goals high and fight hard to accomplish them.

Understand hard times are just that—hard times—and they produce hardworking people. Know that, in the end, the hard times will pass, and you will stand victorious! God made human beings to be incredible and to be able to do amazing things, in which they have super potential. After all, He did make us in His own image. Imagine doing great things, and you will! The more you dream, the more you should live to accomplish your dreams. Have the courage to go after whatever you believe with everything in you!

Surround yourself with people smarter than yourself. Build good relationships; they will improve your state of thinking and eliminate loneliness. Set values for yourself, and don't break them. Remember that setting values for yourself will help you understand what kind of person you are. It is important for you to know who you are as a person so you will know where you want to be in life and how you are going to get there based on your skill sets. Again, know yourself inside and out and meditate daily on your weaknesses and strengths. This will help you understand what to improve on and what to sharpen so as to make certain things about yourself even more refined and more effective.

Remember prayer changes things. Put God in all your plans; He is truly "The Wonderful Counselor" who will advise you and see you through the fog, so that you can reach your most sought after aspirations. Acknowledge God in all your ways, and He shall direct your paths (KJV).

Believe in yourself and in the power of God's timing, and He will see you through. Many times, more often than not, we want to rush our goals and dreams. Nevertheless, we are all on His time and not ours. There is an old quote from an unknown author that says, "If you want to hear God laugh, tell him what you have planned"; hence to say go after your dreams but don't worry about when and how it's going to take place. Simply put your dream in God's hands, and He'll take it from there, while you do the necessary work to complete your goal. In other words, while pursing your positive goals, there are going to be obstacles that you will see as you continue on your journey that you know that you can't do anything about at the moment. This is where you let God come in and take over, yielding to His infinitely wise strategy.

Energize yourself with a positive lifestyle of feel-good relationships and a healthy way of eating. You must understand that your friendships and your food are critical elements that you will take into your mind, body, soul, and spirit. Believe me, they will affect you either for the better or for the worse. Choose wisely!

How To Begin and
Where To Start

PREFACE

The psychology of being "trapped to succeed" is a new branch of success psychology that is comprised of other branches of psychology that came before it: (1) behavioral neuroscience, (2) cognitive psychology/cognitive behavioral therapy, (3) developmental psychology, (4) educational psychology, (5) gestalt psychology, (6) health psychology, (7) moral psychology, (8) neuropsychology, (9) positive psychology, (10) Psychotherapy, (11) social psychology. However, it should be noted that the "psychology of being trapped to succeed" created by Eric F. Prince, although comprised of other elements from branches of psychology that came before it, provides *new insights* into how the human mind works with regard to being successful by processing and initiating systematic actions that will cause one to be successful.

It is also important to point out that the author's empirical observations involve various situations from varied periods on overcoming obstacles and gaining success that are based on a longitudinal, retrospective, research case studies of his personal experiences that provide valuable insight into becoming trapped to succeed! This longitudinal research study spans over twenty years, and the evidence has been overwhelmingly saturated and substantiated. This is important because it provides evidence that the research presented is based on rigorous investigation of competent data analysis which is a critical component of how the scientific community presents non-erroneous data to their peers and the public which shows competency in psychological practice for maximum achievement development levels (Fouad et al., 2009; Kaslow, 2004; Kaslow et al., 2009; National Academy of Sciences, 2009; NCSPP, 2007).

This is why there is no other branch of success psychology such as this most recent edition of success psychology which I have called "trapped to succeed." There is no other branch of psychology that promotes the human populace to become "trapped to succeed" or locked into success by combining a mixture of the psychological branches and subdivisions of psychology, such as psychotherapy interventions and/or terms of psychology to propel the human race into becoming and being "trapped to succeed." Nevertheless, it was necessary, ethical, and prudent for me to give credit, acknowledgment, and recognition to those branches of psychology that came before "success psychology" and to the greatest psychologist of them all, the one true Lord, Christ, who without His eternal wisdom, there would be no field of psychology where psychological practice would be able to prevail in human affairs by assisting mankind in their endeavors with mental wellness, wholeness, and soundness of mind. This is why Christ stated in His word, "Let this mind be in you, which is also in Christ Jesus" (Philippians 2:5, KJV).

For if we as humans allow this mental process to take place in our minds as Christ stated where he said, "Let this mind be in you, which was also in Christ Jesus," the possibilities will be endless. Dr. Joel Paris made a valid argument in his book *The Intelligent Clinicians Guide To The DSM*, in which he stated that we are decades away when it comes to understanding the brain and that although one's mind depends on the brain, the mind cannot be entirely reduced to the activity of neurons in the human brain which are somewhere in the billions numerically (Paris, 2015, pp. 20–21). This is why it is not only Dr. Joel Paris who understands the need to differentiate one's mind from the brain to some degree, but also other scientific researchers who state that there is a need to be clear in the distinction between psychological disorders and neurological disorders which are diverse in nature (Bondi, 1992). A good example is where one can observe two equally healthy people with properly functioning brains, but both of them have their minds made up to do something totally different, where one person's choice will lead to the destruction of his/her brain and the other to the growth and further development of his/her brain for greater levels of growth and success. This is why the conceptualization of mental disorders, as supposed to mental illness, should be based on competence and not just mere pathologizing of an individual according to the *Diagnostic and Statistical Manual of Mental Disorders* (5th ed., DSM-5, American Psychiatric Association [APA], 2013; Bondi, 1992).

This provokes me to make this statement because we are decades away from understanding the brain; the best thing to do would be to allow Christ Himself to enter one's mind and provide one with the nurture and care that it needs which will ultimately be the best source of help that one can ask for on a psychological level. Even if we possessed great amounts of data about the brain, which we do, we will never completely understand the brain the way the creator does; therefore, "it's best to stay humble" (Paris, 2015). I am, therefore, thankful for the statement by Dr. Joel Paris because it shows transparency in the field of psychology and within its subdivisions, especially in those areas of psychiatry, clinical psychology, and forensic psychology.

FURTHER RESEARCH DATA AND GENERAL INFORMATION

It is critical to note that I discovered a *problem* when it comes to many human beings being successful on what they would consider large scales. The problem is that there are many humans who do not know how to go about achieving their goals or how to overcome the fears that are correlated with their goals. *What we know* about success is that success is attainable if one puts forth the effort to achieve various types of success. *What we do not know* is that there are and can be very complex subdivisions of success along with very sophisticated methods that one must apply to oneself to obtain success. These methods have not yet been tapped into by a great portion of societal members because of lack of knowledge. Therefore, *there is a gap* in the research of becoming successful. This book seeks to answer the *research question*: How can one become trapped to succeed?

The *methodologies* that have been utilized in this book have been implemented to answer the research question (How does one become trapped to succeed?) and are derived from the following: longitudinal, retrospective case studies, and *data analysis* that have been collected and that are based on evidence-based research that is descriptive, exploratory, phenomenological, and qualitative in scientific research, which involves real-life short stories on the personal empirical experiences of the author and one-on-one interviews and focus groups ascertained from a multitude of various types of professional people from different settings (e.g., researchers, doctors, police officers, professional actors, pastors, educators, and other notable people).

It is also very critical to note that the main methodology utilized from a qualitative approach was that of the *triangulation methodology*. This investigates more than one source to substantiate and validate a claim that is being made and/or to produce an understanding. Again, I utilized real-life short stories from the personal empirical experiences of the author and one-on-one interviews that are ascertained from various professional people. The people interviewed are from various settings who have, without controversy, failed many times in their lives but overcame their trials and went on to become successful. I am one of those people, and I can tell you now I have failed over and over and over again! For every one of my successes, there have been countless failures, but I did not give up, and you must not give up as well.

Below are just two examples of what a triangulation data image would look like if one were to see it visually. Other images can be more complex in nature, scope, and sequence.

Figure no. 1

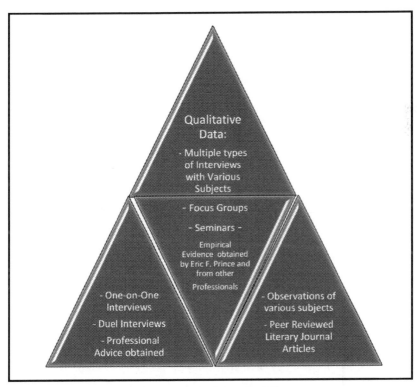

Figure no. 2, July 24, 2018

It is critical to understand that when an individual reads a substantial number of books, talks to a large number of people, and the information that is received is constantly the same, then this is when you have saturated the investigation and can come to the conclusion based on those multiple sources that the question that is being asked or the thing that is being investigated is most likely to be valid and true. Nevertheless, one should make sure that the sources that are being investigated are credible in nature and that they can be trusted to provide accurate data or information. This is why one should talk to and interview a person or people who are still currently or have been for a long time engaged in the element that they are investigating; this will most likely produce accurate, honest results. If asked a general question about their experiences, most people will tell the truth about what they have seen, heard, or experienced, unless they are in fear of retribution or some sort of negative consequence. For example, if I ask ten people on a sunny day, when the sun is shining brightly, "Is the sun out?" all ten will most likely say yes.

The data analysis repeatedly revealed that one can become trapped to succeed on a large scale if they follow certain criteria in this book for success. This book is not the end all, be all of how to go about being successful majority of the time. However, it does present a very robust case on the subject matter of success and how to become trapped to succeed. Furthermore, its contents present data that should not be ignored as it pertains to success. It is also not for the unbelieving or the faint of heart but, rather, for those who are truly sick and tired of the traditional ways of doing things. This book is for those who are willing to open their minds to new insights and revelations from what the data reveal, which can and will propel them into new heights of growth and development with greater ratios of success. It should be noted that this book is written so as to attract all people.

Therefore, it is not a traditional book but, rather, a multifaceted book, in which its contents are based on the premise of a self-help book but also that of diverse research methodologies stemming from qualitative analysis, case studies, phenomenological scientific explanations, new insights and revelations for practitioners and others, empirical observations and other forms of research data to captivate and inspire all readers. I ask that the scientific community understand this as this book, a self-help book, is written to help the masses but also to be presented as a scientific guide such that it meets the guidelines of responsible conduct in research which is the goal of those who represent the scientific community (American Psychological Association 2010; American Psychological Association, 2015; National Academy of Sciences 2009).

PERSONAL NOTE TO YOU, THE READER

The below message is for you, the reader, to say with *passion* every day on a *metacognitive level* while you work toward your goal(s)! Watch yourself transform into a new, greater you! *Metacognition* is defined as "the awareness an individual has of their own mental processes" (Oxford University Press, 2015); in other words, how you think about thinking. The prefix "meta" means to *change* and/or *transform* which is what this book will cause you to do. In some cases, the word *meta* even means *beyond*; for instance, to go beyond your normal way of thinking. *Cognition*, however, is defined as the mental action or process of acquiring knowledge and understanding through one's thoughts, experiences, and senses.

Through this book, you can enter into a realm where your normal mental process goes beyond your normal way of thinking and where your actions will be transformed from normal actions to actions that are done purposefully and systematically which will allow you to become trapped to succeed! It should also be noted that writings on metacognition can be traced back to as far as De Anima and the Parva Naturalia of the Greek philosopher Aristotle (384–322 BC), and that the phenomenon was brought to prominence during the 1970's largely by the U.S. psychologist John H(urley) Flavell (born 1928) who focused attention, especially on developmental aspects of metacognition (Oxford Reference, n.d). The metamorphose process of becoming trapped to succeed begins in 3, 2, 1 . . .

Every day repeat the following:

I will not stop until I overcome every obstacle, climb every personal mountain, conquer my every dream! I will become *trapped to succeed!*

I understand the road will get rough sometimes, but I will not stand here and let my dreams pass me by. I will learn how to become trapped to succeed in life!

THE

ROLE

OF

MOTIVATION

AND

HOW

TO STAY MOTIVATED

Chapter 1

The Importance Of Staying Motivated

Motivation—how and why it's important to stay motivated. When we look at the word *motivated*, what comes to the mind of the person who's actually trying to get motivated or stay motivated? Let's be realistic, what are they thinking? What's going on in the mind of that person who is sitting there contemplating when he or she is going to get charged up enough to begin working on that dream or that goal that they have thought about for so long? Let me assist you in understanding this process. Number 1, you are going to have to see yourself engaging that goal or that dream. Motivation comes from the desire that you truly want something badly enough to actually put some blood, sweat, and tears into what you are trying to accomplish. Let's take for instance this book you're reading right now, a book that took me twenty years to finish, because if I really wanted the book to have a positive outcome on people's lives, it would have to be based on solid empirical evidence which would take time to gather as it is based on a retrospective, longitudinal, research case studies.

This evidence would lead me into the journey of conducting a longitudinal study which took extreme motivation for it to become a reality. Many times I didn't feel like sitting down to type with everything else that I had going on. However, I knew I had to get started. It was late, and I had just gotten off work from standing on my feet all day. Nevertheless, I was determined not to put it off any longer. It was late in the night, about 1:50 a.m. And I had not been to sleep at all since I had gotten home. I was tired, and my eyes were burning, but the motivation was having an audience of people to have a book signing for and the self- gratification of being a first-time author. However, years later, I wrote a spy thriller titled *Agent 008: The Untold Story*, and someone told me that I should put out *Trapped to Succeed* second to show that I had something that I had succeeded in. It hurt to hear that, but that person was right.

I needed to wait to put this book out so as to establish credibility as one who had been successful. Thus, I was thrust into a longitudinal study that I really didn't want to be in, but for the sake of those people (mankind) I wanted to help become trapped to succeed, it was a necessary evil that the longitudinal study on myself be conducted.

I never dreamed that I would ever have a chance to write my own book, or books for that matter. However, again, I was motivated by the thought that there was a publishing company out there that would give me my first break. This is how you must think. You must believe that where there is a will, there is a way. You must remember that if you put your mind to it, it may take some time, but you will get there! You will arrive at your destination victorious! You must believe that there is some form of possibility in the world that will at some point present itself and that you will never give up until it does. This is how great minds think!

Do you have a great mind? If you didn't, I can tell right now that there is a high probability that you would not be reading this book on how to become trapped to succeed. The mere fact that you are reading this book means you took the time to develop yourself by investing in reading where you would learn from someone who has carved the way before you. Good job! And kudos to you!

Be honest with yourself—if you say you really want something, do you sit there and wait for it to come to you, or do you get go after it with everything in you the way a dog goes after that T-bone steak after a hard day's work in the field or as a professional football player who's been playing in the sun all day and observing the last fresh cold drink of ice water sitting on the table who knocks over all his teammates to get to it first? I mean, come on, let's be serious, do you really want it, or are you just saying you want it? Because if you're just saying you want it, believe me, you'll know because you'll never get it! If you are not motivated, it's not going to happen for you!

Whatever it is, you must understand that motivation not only comes from other people, but it also come from within, it is intrinsic, which, in my opinion, is the best kind of motivation to have because you don't have to worry about people trying to motivate you. Yes, I'm talking about you—wake up! The people who always have to have external motivation that stems from other people giving it to them have a more difficult time being or staying motivated. Most people have a hard time staying motivated themselves, let alone trying to motivate someone else, unless you are going to go to motivational speaker seminars all the time. You are the architect of your dreams! You must understand that it is you who creates the blueprint for your success. Once you understand this factor, you will be well on your way to becoming trapped to succeed. It's only fair that I tell you the truth. So get over other people motivating you and learn how to be internally motivated, and I can promise, you will see a strong, positive difference in your life as it relates to your accomplishments!

It is important that you understand that you are your worst enemy or your best friend, and sometimes you have to be there to say to yourself "Yes, I can do this!" and get up and attack your goal, your dream, with everything in you, if you want to accomplish it. Instead of sitting there waiting for friends or family to tell you that you can do it, or that, if they had your talent they would be rich by now, get up and get started on your goal. The truth is we have all had that said to us one time or another. Then we begin to say to ourselves "Yeah, yeah, one day I'm going to do it," and then we never do. I'm telling you the facts about how things happen on the way to being successful so that you can see the difference of how you *don't want* to be as supposed to how you *really want to be.*

It is important to learn what motivates you and once you know, to never let that power go. As we explore our minds and get our neurotransmitters fired up to stay motivated, which will help us unlock the secrets of what causes us to excel or what motivates us to want to succeed, one must remember that different things motivate different people; some people are motivated by the love of family or friends, some are motivated by music, others by the encouraging words of an inspirational speaker.

Regardless of what it is that motivates you, you must get it down to a science and begin the quest of seeking deep inside yourself to discover what truly causes motivation in you so that you can use it every day as a springboard propelling you into greater levels of success toward your ultimate goal. You must understand that success comes in degrees before the goal can be fully realized. To accomplish anything, you must know yourself—your likes, your dislikes, your weaknesses, and your strengths. It is critical to know yourself internally and externally. Motivation is an untapped power that many people already have stored inside them which stems from things that they love.

They only need to tap into that power. What motivation does is what can be described as how vitamins affect the human body. Motivation provides you with energy, only without the pill but you still get the energy and the self-drive to accomplish the task you have at hand. As a person with innate feelings and emotions, you know and understand how you feel when you get that surge of energy that causes you to become instantaneously determined to achieve something that you automatically know in your heart and mind that nothing is going to stop you. Ask yourself, "What it is that is in me that caused me to feel this way? What gave me the self-drive and the mental and physical desire to want to go after that goal with everything in me?" Whatever it was, once you find out the source of your motivation, hold on to it, and do everything you can to preserve it within you so that you can accomplish your goals consistently!

It is that special miraculous feeling from within that tells you no matter what comes or what goes, you can and will overcome and be a success in everything that you put your mind to do because you are motivated by the number one motivator who will always be there for you—yourself! And the God-given ability to be self-motivated and self-driven is something that no one can take from you.

The importance of staying motivated is just as important as staying healthy. Your success depends on the depth of your motivation or self-determination, just as the outcome of your life is dependent on your state of health. If one element is off balance, it can destroy your goals and/or deter you from a positive outcome in life. Therefore, with this in mind, one should put forth a great effort to increase their levels of motivation from within.

Majority of us have heard the term at one point or another that what a person puts into life is what they will get out. That's a strong motivating factor right there. Personally, I can get a self-high and increase my neurological dopamine levels just thinking about all the possibilities that are out there for me to accomplish. Yes, it will take work, and there will be obstacles, but doesn't success and positive growth feel good? Isn't it worth it?

I remember personally hearing the words "What you put in life is what you'll get out!" When I heard this, I became like a child in a candy store, imagining all the possibilities of becoming successful at anything and everything. The "wow factor" began to hit me big time! I thought to myself, *You mean to tell me that whatever I put into life is what I will get out?* My answer to that thought was *Okay, I'll just put everything in that I can so that I can complete every goal, overcome every obstacle, climb every mountain, swim every valley! Just do it all! I'll just do everything that I can and dream big.* I believe you know and understand what I'm talking about, that young ambition and zeal that motivated individuals get when they first get that idea to achieve something. The thing is to keep that motivation and not let it run out because of the pressures in life and the normal struggles that a day can bring. It's all stressful and tiring, and then you, with your ambitious self, had to go and take on a new challenge. Well, let me inform you it's normal—all successful people go through that phase. That's the phase of being tried and tested, where if the person passes, they will begin to become molded and crystallized in what they are doing, where they will become as pure as gold.

It is also a difficult process to find gold in gold mines and then to make the gold look remarkable. It's also a difficult process to take a field of grapes and turn them into fine wine. It doesn't happen overnight, but when it does happen, and the evolutionary process is complete, the taste is out of sight! That's why when you finish suffering, after all the pain and sacrifice, you get to eat the breakfast of champions. That's why people come to you and say

"Keep up the good work!" or "How do you do it? What motivates you? What keeps you so driven to do what you do?" Those times, seeing your hard work turn into self-satisfying accomplishments, will be undoubtedly some of the best times of your life!

The feeling of self-gratification is a beautiful thing, not to mention the big bank accounts, the CEO license plates, and other perks that you personally earned because you were willing to go through the storm and the fire. Although sometimes you were tired, you still maintained motivation from within, from *God* who is the source of it all!

You went through the rough times, and now look where you are, all because you kept persisting, praying, staying motivated, believing in yourself, and getting on your knees to say those prayers. Now you are at the top of the mountain, which, at one point, was so far off. You are the king of your hill because you searched for and found that link, that element, that started it all and enabled you to finish it all! You explored yourself and discovered the skill of how to become constantly motivated from within!

*C*hapter 2

The Methods of Staying Motivated

So, when we weigh the pros and the cons about the learning of self and understanding one's self as far as what turns you on, or what turns you off? what makes you cold? or what makes you hot? What puts you in the heat of the moment every time you get a fresh goal, and keeps you there? The question must be asked— how does one stay motivated every time an individual gets a desire to accomplish something and the individual knows it's going to be a tough situation at hand and the person does not want to lose that desire that he/she created, or his/her ambition later down the line? The pros far outweigh the cons when it comes to the investment of learning yourself, which can be done by journaling your most negative and positive inner feelings about life and then strategically working to improve yourself where you modify your behavioral patterns. In the field of psychology, we call this cognitive behavioral therapy. My suggestion to you is that you remember that positive feeling that you had when you first became inspired by that vision of success that caused you to get all heated up and that made you feel all warm and fuzzy on the inside, just the way that first date you had with that beautiful woman or that handsome hunk! This is another tactic of staying motivated—remembering what it was that started the romance in the first place. Let's think about it for a minute. Why do you continue a love affair with anything or anybody? What is in it for you? What are you getting out of it?

These are some of the things you need to tell yourself to keep yourself motivated. You should try picturing visually the outcome of whatever it is you have set out to accomplish so that it teases you into working toward reaching and obtaining whatever it is you are hoping for. In fact, if you keep seeing it, you'll want it more and more, and you'll get the motivation from within to get it. This is what makes you resilient, never stopping, although you may encounter difficulties that attempt to deter you from reaching your goals. If it takes you getting into or delving into a spiritual plane with the creator to keep yourself motivated, a little prayer every now and then won't hurt. God is the big boss anyway! Some psychologists utilize faith-based practices in the process of therapy to assist clients in achieving their goals for better lives. If you have to pray, fast, meditate, workout, or start eating healthier, do whatever it takes to accomplish your goals, dreams, or desires—just get it done!

Hopefully, you'll utilize positive methods, but sometimes, even when you remain positive, you will still have to be relentless in your pursuit in a positive way, and nothing's wrong with that! Being motivated and staying motivated is a gift in itself; people who are optimistic even respond to people who are positively motivated. When people observe that you are motivated, they cling to you like magnets and for good reason.

In my strong opinion, and one that is based on empirical evidence, meaning I have repeatedly observed this phenomena in various situations and settings, being positive, optimistic, and motivational is like being a celebrity— people want to follow you and celebrate you! It is almost as if you are a celebrity because almost everyone wants to be a part of that positive energy that you are radiating from your inner person. It's just something about that man or woman who possesses the power of being able to uplift and strengthen another human being, their fellow man, who may be down, and almost out of nowhere, they have the ability to lift them up! (Which one are you?)

Some might agree that there is nothing better than that nature of having self-motivation, also known as intrinsic motivation, because right then, at that very moment when you start thinking on your goal rather long term or short term, you can feel it, taste it, and almost even touch it! Right now, some of you are probably saying "Where is he taking me?" and I can tell you I am taking you to a point where if you can constantly capture the essence of being self-motivated and stay in the mind frame of being motivated, then you'll enter into a dimension where there is an unlimited access to success, a dimension where there are no boundaries to achievement, a place in time and space where the power of motivation is unstoppable, and you are chief explorer. This is God's will through His Son! This is His gift to you! It is to see you live a life of great abundance and joy! (John 10:10, KJV)

I am not saying you will not see troubles along the way or sorrows at different points in your life, but if you can stay motivated, positive, and pray for resilience, you will make it through. If you recall earlier, I mentioned how different people are motivated by different things. One thing that I cannot leave out is the fact that some people get motivated by anger, and if that's what it takes to get you motivated, so be it! I believe that sometimes the emotion of anger may be what it takes to get the ball rolling in your life. What kind of anger am I speaking of? I am speaking of the type of anger that you get tired of being a failure and decide to stand up for yourself and fight for what you want, even if it means fighting yourself! You should know that sometimes you will have to fight for yourself to align your body with your heart, soul, and mind.

It is also important to know that you must fight the negativity that may surround you, such as people who don't like or don't want to see you in a motivated state of mind. Remember, and take this very seriously, there are some people who are and will be happy for you, and there are some people who are not and will not be happy for you.

You should always be careful who you tell your plans to for this very reason; there are people out there who don't want to see you make it, so therefore, you should keep your business to yourself when in doubt of whom you are talking to. These are negative factors that will suck your motivation right out of your soul and you are trying to stay motivated. It is sometimes, if not all the time, good to keep your personal goals to yourself.

Are you not the person in charge of your affairs or what your future or your destiny is going to be? Discernment of people using wisdom is a critical key to success! Wisdom is the application of knowledge. This is something that we most often let other people in on, our aspirations in life, and then unfortunately and to our demise, we find out that they could careless and, even worse, sometimes may not be happy to hear of your positive plans and, if they could, drain all your motivation. Get away from them as quickly as you can! You can pray for them, but get away because if they drain you of your positivity, you will be rendered incapable of helping yourself, or anyone else for that matter, stay motivated.

Okay, take a moment to breath for a second. Now get over the shock! It's true, but not all have to go through this scenario. Some friends can be very motivational and encouraging! Nevertheless, I feel that no matter who is jealous of you, if you put the good Lord, God, first in your life, and if you are truly motivated to accomplish something, nothing can stop you but yourself. All you have to do is take charge! Stop looking down, and look up! Believe in yourself, and keep thinking positive! I know personally, with all these characteristics, you will not fail! Sometimes you just have to roll with the punches, go through the many changes, and deal with the obstacles in life! The Bible says, "So as a man thinketh, so is he" (Proverbs 3:7, KJV).

This applies to the entire human populace. If you think you are a failure, chances are you are going to fail. If you think you are a success, you will be a success! It's all up to you! Learn how to be an inspiration and motivation to yourself first, and then you can be an inspiration and a motivation to others, which is where the real success comes into play. It is a healthy mentality to desire and to learn more about ourselves, to learn new ways to constantly have inner motivation and optimistic thought patterns that increase neurocognition growth which will allow and expand the brain's neuroplasticity levels to discover new ways to do new and exciting things.

Learning new things about yourself helps the brain to reorganize itself to understand how to stay motivated and accomplish your goals in a more systematic way and effective way. The average person would be surprised how much the brain can expand, grow, and retain highly-substantial amounts of data even in adulthood.

For example, a positive conversation that brings upon new learning experiences will have a high probability of expanding the brain. A good reference point is two of my favorite textbooks that discuss neuroscience as it relates to brain growth. The first book is titled *Intentional Interviewing and Counseling*, in which according to Ivey, Ivey, and Zalaquett, in their section on "Neuro Science, the Brain, and Counseling," where they state that "Whether in interviewing, counseling, or psychotherapy, the conversation changes the brain through the development of new neural networks" (2014, p. 21). This is a good example of how brain plasticity works.

The second textbook titled *Applied Helping Skills* discusses the dynamics of neuroplasticity by simply stating that "If a person is pushed or motivated, then they will profit from the encounter that they experienced" (Brew & Kottler, 2008, p. 17). I can tell you firsthand that you will profit because your brain will grow with the newfound motivation and stimulation, thereby increasing positive work activity. This is why it is important to take your vitamins! For instance, vitamin B-12 and vitamin D are extremely important to your brain. The reason being is the fact that these vitamins assist human beings in maintaining their psychological balance while simultaneously preserving the protective myelin in your brain and nerve cells as documented by Tufan et al. (2012)

This is why it is important at all times to engulf oneself with positive things and people that increase the brain's neuroplasticity levels. It is important to stay motivated, stay positive, and stay healthy! One way of staying motivated is by understanding the knowledge of oneself because doing so will ultimately cause you to have the most wonderful kind of success in your life by simply understanding that you can achieve anything that you put your mind to and how to go about doing it.

Taking care of the brain is important because poor maintenance of the brain can adversely affect your societal and interpersonal relationships that you will need to build strong foundations for future success (Berk, 2010). This leads me to a critical point that you must understand: Eating the correct foods and taking the proper vitamins is vital to the healthy neurocognitive functioning of your brain. There are countless scientific research studies from my peers in the scientific community in psychological practice and in neuroscience that prove this theory which should not be overlooked.

For instance, in one research study conducted by researchers from the Department of Physiology, Anatomy, and Genetics at the University of Oxford. They alert societal members to the fact that vitamin B-12 is critical in keeping, further developing, and preventing the loss of brain deterioration (Vogiatzoglou et al., 2008). Lent (2004) also makes it very clear that we as humans should take a practical approach to our psycho (Mental) social adjustments where the human perspective to well-being is constantly evolving for the better. Keeping oneself mentally healthy is vital, which is why the (American Board of Psychiatry and Neurology, 2007) highly support academic and public awareness on progressive brain health. Needless to say, taking care of oneself is a major contributing factor to long-term success, and the high maintenance of the mind, body, and soul are key factors in the process of becoming trapped to succeed!

The brain's amygdala is directly connected to overcoming fear, regulating human emotion, and assisting human beings who are unmotivated become motivated. Now a brief neuroscience lesson: Recent findings provide critical data/information that alerts those who seek to have high levels of mental health functionality that *dietary factors* exert their effects on the brain by affecting molecular events related to the *management of energy metabolism* and that of synaptic plasticity which is another way of saying helping your brains neural transmitters (courier express mail delivery) continue to grow and expand its network within your brain. In other words, the more energy metabolism influences the brain's neuronal functioning, neuronal signaling, and synaptic plasticity, the more one's mental health will be positively increased which will ultimately affect their motivation levels.

Now before I move on; I want to also point out that the epigenetic regulation of neuronal plasticity has been documented by scientists to be a critical system of the brain's amygdala by which, if proper foods and vitamins are a part of your diet, it can prolong their effects on long-term neuronal plasticity, which means one will have longevity in healthy brain functioning, which also means that he/she will have higher levels of plasma membrane function, intraneuronal signaling, and learning cognition according to Gomez-Pinella and Tyagi (2013). Earlier, if you recall, I mentioned that vitamin B-12 and vitamin D are great vitamins that assist your brain in healthy neuro functioning; now here is another vitamin to add to the list, and that vitamin is none other than that of the omega-3 fatty acid vitamin according to Gomez-Pinella (2008) and Gomez-Pinella and Tyagi (2013).

There are many important things that a person needs to remember when putting forth the effort to stay motivated. One thing for sure is that for every positive, there is a negative, and for every negative, there is a positive. The key is to not allow the negatives to outweigh the positives because they can eventually get the best of you. For instance, you are motivated to do something, but then the minute you attempt to act on the inspiration, here comes something negative to deter you or stop you. Now when I use the word *negative*, this could mean an obstacle in front of you; this obstacle could be yourself, another person, time, or events. It's often never just one thing! However, regardless of what it is, you have to make up in your mind that you are bigger than that mountain, that your faith in yourself, in God, and in your God-given capabilities will see you through.

I personally believe that if you don't move the mountain, they stay right there, and you will forever remain in a state of being where you know that it must be done! If this is not important to you, I don't know what is. No one wants mountains in their life that will always hold them back from being successful.

You must understand that you are man or woman enough to climb the mountains that God allowed to be placed in front of you, that He would not place a burden upon you that you are unable to bear. You will be successful because you are an overcomer, and the one proof of it is the fact that you are reading this book. You are ahead of the race! You must tell yourself that "If another person can make it, so can I. I breathe, bleed, drink, eat, and sleep the same way another human being does, and I am willing to put the same amount of work in that they put in, if not more, so that I too can be successful!" The equation that you have to figure out is, how are you going to stay motivated? You must constantly search for away! Whether mental, physical, spiritual, or all three of these life domains, you must stay in shape.

I prefer to stay strong in the realm of all three life domains, and I suggest that you do too. Nevertheless, it's up to you to determine your own destiny with the mind frame you have or will have after reading this book which will determine the amount of work you put in. Staying motivated is critical to a person's livelihood. Believe it or not, one even has to be motivated to do nothing. However, God put other human beings on earth to motivate other human beings and inspire them to do great things!

Using other people as motivating factors can serve as a useful strategy on your road to success! There is no need to be jealous of another human being. Great human beings are human just as you are; the only difference is they seized opportunities by getting up and working hard to accomplish their goals where others would not have dreamed to put the amount of exhaustive hours in that those who became successful put in. Furthermore, they did not allow the fear of success to consume them and stop them from acting upon their goals. If you are going to be afraid, be afraid of failure.

The fear you need to have is the fear that if you don't stop being afraid, you may never accomplish your goals and become unsuccessful. Many people have experienced it since living on this earth, and what they have experienced is that with motivation came the ability to have faith. A person cannot have motivation without faith; they go hand in hand. If you are motivated to do something, this means you have faith. For faith drives motivation! As you continue along this journey of becoming trapped to succeed, it is very important that you remember life is beautiful!

And accomplishing your goals, dreams, and aspirations, although they may be challenging, will be worth living for on this earth. So with this, I say unto you stand up to circumstances, situations, problems, obstacles, pressures, doubts, which all fall right up under that nasty word *fear*. Fear can be used negatively or positively. However, when "fear" is trying to stand in the way of your dreams, that is a negative fear. The fear of God is good. God tells us to fear Him for a good reason. If you were afraid to get on the bike when your parent or guardian took the training wheels off, you would have never learned to ride the bike. In other words, people have to let go of fear to accomplish certain goals. There will be times when you are bruised or banged up while you are fighting to achieve your goals. This is what separates the winners from the rest of those in race. I can tell you now, don't give up; accomplishing your goals during hardships will be something you will always have to do.

A good example of overcoming fear can be learned from reading this very brief but real account that happened to me on overcoming fear and how I used fear against fear in reference to my success as an actor. I won't go into it too much because you'll read about it later in this book. However, what I want to share with you is how I was able to get into the Screen Actors Guild, the professional union that many actors want to get into. Once an aspiring actor is in the union, they have obtained a level of status that is recognized throughout the world. Those who take acting seriously know about the Screen Actors Guild.

This story starts out when I was on the set of *Light It Up* the movie! I kept telling myself I'm not supposed to go up and talk to the directors or the producers about speaking roles. Nevertheless, I kept telling myself if I don't, I will be an extra all my life! I was determined not to let that happen because acting is one of the things I love to do and is going to be successful at doing. The one thing that an aspiring actor is told not to do on the set is ask the directors, or anyone for that matter, for a speaking role.

This is a seriously frowned-upon thing to do when you are on the set, especially when you are a budding actor/actress. If you ask the wrong person, one could end up getting kicked off the set and his/her name thrown, dragged through the mud to other people, such as casting directors; so believe me when I tell you I was very afraid of going against the grain. On the other hand, I was more afraid of not stepping up and believing in myself, and not asking for a speaking role, which could have resulted in me being an extra all my life. The time was now!

I used the fear of failure and/or being a "wanna-be" film actor all my life as a method of motivation to force myself to act on my great desire to get into the Screen Actors Guild. I knew this would take perfect timing. I gathered myself and became more confident in that moment, and there it was—the moment had arrived—this executive producer going to kick me off the set or, worse, get my name and bad-mouth me to other producers and casting directors. I really didn't know what this man was going to do. I stood there looking at this man who had the power to help me or hurt me or significantly slow me down—notice I didn't say "break me." Only God can break me, but God said, "I would that you prosper and be in good health" (3 John 1:2, KJV). I slowly went up to him and popped the question! "Excuse me. My name is Eriq Prince. What's yours?"

He responded by telling me his name. "How can I help you?" he said.

I took my time to formulate my words and say, "I was hoping you could give me a speaking role in this movie so I could go to Hollywood and audition for movies because I'm aware of the fact that you need to be in the Screen Actors Guild to audition for major movies in Hollywood."

I became very quiet and still and began to listen intently to what his response was going to be out of fear of rejection. I stood there literally shaking in my boots because it was winter and I was very nervous. It seemed like hours in my mind but was actually only a few seconds when he gave his response, which was "I can do that, I understand. Sure, no problem." I could not believe my ears! I was in a state of shock and pure happiness at the same time. I reflected on the praying, the fasting, the meditating, and the anguish of trying to find out who was going to help me.

I remembered wondering for days who was going to help me, who do I ask, when do I ask, and where do I ask. Sometimes success is about the right timing. Nevertheless, I asked, even though I was nervous, and it paid off! I must say again it took prayer, timing social skills, and patience, but it happened! All the pain and sacrifice was worth it! I remember the executive producer saying, "Let's set up over here for a speaking role with Mr. Eriq F. Prince!" It was one of the most beautiful things that I had ever heard in my life! I had overcome a problem that destroys dreams, and that problem is the fear of trying! I had successfully used fear as a method to stay motivated and not fall victim to fear.

I was more afraid of being a failure than being humiliated, and it paid off. It took about a month of standing around and waiting, but I was determined to make it through the storm! I was determined to sign those SAG contracts! Upon doing so, I felt a feeling of success and achievement! It was extremely rewarding. Staying motivated and having a method, which was constant belief in myself, and having faith in my creator had paid off! Now I was on my way to using my celebrity status to do what I was brought in the world to do, which is to help others, especially those from broken homes and impoverished upbringings.

There are so many children who have never seen the world, so many children who have never visited a museum and/or done other things to enrich their lives, because they just do not have the resources. I was, and still am, determined to change this negative fact to some degree. My celebrity power would provide me with a powerful springboard in which to infuse the next generation with power through teaching them about the concept of resilience that which I was determined to be a powerful motivating factor that would affect positive change. Krovetz (2008), in his textbook titled *Fostering Resilience*, under the subsection "Managing Change," discusses the fact that "change is external and situational" (p. 128).

Krovetz defines *transition* as the *psychological process* every human being goes through to adjust to change, which makes it an internal process. This is critical to understand because when I was going through my *psychological process* and dealing with the fears of rejection as I made my transition into the world of professional acting in 2002, I was writing the book that you are reading now. Through my book *Trapped to Succeed*, I was determined to make a change in my life, so as to make a positive, effective, dynamic change in the lives of others. My method of motivation had become bigger than myself, and I was now becoming a person who wanted to motivate others! I wanted to show them how to become trapped to succeed. I had no idea that the book *How to Become Trapped to Succeed* would turn into a new branch of psychology called success psychology!

It is critical for me to explain to those who read this book that the sole purpose of this book is to infuse the reader with knowledge from various aspects of literature and other forms of data, whether it be from the life experiences of others or through my own life experiences taken from that of a retrospective case study that are based on real-life empirical evidence that caused me pain, hardship, and/or great happiness, where the goal is to assist the readers in understanding themselves on a whole new level and where they can apply psychological, physiological elements in their own lives that will stimulate the mind by way of the brain and increase the productivity of the readers' neural network when it comes to setting goals and completing them. The writer's motivation for writing this book stems from the fact that he believes that he can and will motivate those who are seeking to be motivated and that he can and will positively change someone's life for the better.

Success psychology is a mixture of critical data that if followed properly can have a high probability of causing success in one's life in any way, shape, form, or fashion. This is why there will be other books under the new branch of success psychology to follow that the writer will contribute to society at large which will be tailored to specific needs of the human populace. The data disseminated will be collected by way of intensive research from the scientific community, peer-reviewed literature, public interviews, as well as mixed methodologies that use case studies; observational studies; quantitative, qualitative, and retrospective studies among other research methodologies.

Whatever method is utilized, it will be indicated in the book. The American Psychological Association promotes *competence* and *ethics* within the field of psychology which is why the data gathered must come from valid sources that can be scientifically substantiated even in books. This means that there is a sound, systematic way that the data was researched, collected, reviewed, and distributed (American Psychological Association, 2015; American Psychological Association, 2010).

STOP! LOOK!
AND
PAY CLOSE ATTENTION!
ARE YOU JUST SAYING
YOU WANT IT? BECAUSE
IF YOU ARE, YOU'LL
KNOW BECAUSE YOU'LL
NEVER GET IT!

UTILIZING THE COGNITIVE BEHAVIORAL SOCRATIC APPROACH

Below are twelve cognitive behavioral questions that will cause you to critically think! These questions will assist you in discovering whether you really want to complete your goals or not!

→ Do you fall in love all over again every time you discuss your goal?

→ Do you feel incomplete knowing that you have not achieved it yet?

→ Do you keep finding yourself looking for ways to accomplish your goal?

→ Do you go through great pain to reach your goal although it may feel as if it is taking forever?

→ Do you dream about your goal at night and wake to it in the morning?

→ Do you hurt inside because you have not completed your goal yet?

→ Do you find yourself restructuring your life to achieve your goal?

→ Do you find yourself getting angry when someone says you might as well give up?

→ Do you find yourself doing what appears to be anything positively possible to accomplish your goal or dream?

→ Do you find yourself saying, "I'm going to make it! And I'm never, ever, going to give up!"?

→ Do you have long-term plans on achieving your goal, even though you know it will take time?

→ Do you involve God Almighty in the pursuit of your goal and dreams?

There are other questions that can be asked which will assist you in understanding yourself, but you have to ask yourself those questions. You can make a journal for yourself and cross off the questions you are fulfilling, and then put a check by the questions that you need to work on.

If you are serious about whatever it is you are trying to accomplish, get up And put hard work, sweat, and passion into it!

Only then you will see the results!

*C*hapter 3

Organizing
Your
Goals

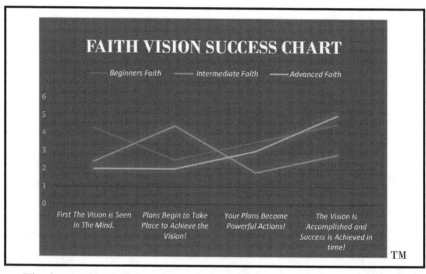

The data in this chart is comprised of the collaborative effort with educator, pastor, chief apostle Dr. Y. B. Amen PhD, chief executive officer and Restorer of Beyth-'El Temple and College and the Church of Yisra-'el

The *faith-vision success chart* has been made so that the readers will be able to observe where they are in obtaining their goals and so they will know what their next step needs to be. It was also done so one can monitor their levels of faith systematically. It is of extreme importance to know where you are in life so you can map out the road ahead. With the help of this chart, you can realistically map out where you are and how close you are to obtaining your goals and being successful.

ORGANIZING YOUR GOALS

So here you are, you've made it this far into the book because you persisted and refused to give up! You've now obtained and learned a few very important secrets on becoming trapped to succeed, but it doesn't stop there. Moving forward, you will learn about organization, why it is important, and why you need to be organized. Organization is an extremely important key to being successful. Without organization, one will not go far. If the person does, it will not last. In the world we live in, we must have some type of method to the madness that we undertake with our goals.

One of my personal methods in being successful is being very, if not extremely, organized. Let's look at the definition of the word *organize*.: According to the Oxford University Press (2015), the word *organize* is described as the following: (1) an organized group of people with a particular purpose, (2) the action of organizing something (3) the quality of being systematic and efficient. In essence, we all want to achieve our objectives; one way of doing that is to have organization skills that will enable us to stay focused, sharp, and on the cutting edge at all times! Organization is very critical to any kind of success, especially in the planning stages.

If you show me an individual who is organized, I will show you an individual who is successful. When one is organized, they will have some type of systematic way of obtaining their goals. There has to be some form of system in place that can be monitored to gauge progress. Organization shows that a person has some type of rational plan to go about achieving their goals. It may not seem rational all the time, and sometimes it may seem as if the person is all over the place, but you never know how they are executing their plan. Sometimes a person's actions may even seem to be full of chaos, but one should understand that there is a concept termed the "chaos theory," where certain actions or events may seem to be random but are rather determined by organized thoughts or preplanned strategies, which are deterministic in nature but are a significant factor to their life's transition (Bussolari & Goodell, 2009; Kiel, Douglas, Elliott, & Euel, 1997).

Think about it for a second or two! How rational can a person be having goals that they want to obtain without being organized? It only takes a few hours of your time to begin the process of being organized; for instance, taking the time to write down your goals with paper and pen or type it up and store it on a flash drive. Goals come with ideas, and ideas have to be harnessed. To harness one's ideas into successful ventures, one must be diligent at keeping records. This can also be done by taking notes through recording one's goals and the steps that they climb to keep things in perspective. For an example, let us take a musician who can come up with great lyrics.

What happens if that musician never writes anything down or is not sure where he left his musical notes and they become lost or destroyed? The result would be, because of his lack of organization, lost information/data that was valuable to the process of his success. For anyone who is in the pursuit of a goal or dream, it would be wise for that person to invest in a small file cabinet for his documents. I could go on and on with examples on being organized, but the truth is if one truly wants to be successful at everything, the essential skill of organization must be realized and utilized in everything so that your goals have a rational means of becoming a reality.

Organizing your goals will definitely help you keep track of things at hand. Another methodology of organizing your goals that I constantly utilize is what my pastor would call a "things-to-do list." A things-to-do list is nothing more than a notebook pad or a piece of paper with things you need to do for the day. I had never seen anybody use that method until him. I had never thought of using that approach. I had always stored things in my mind, which is okay if you can do that effectively and efficiently. However, some people are motivated by sight and are visual learners, and therefore, the same concept applies when actually completing short-term and long-term goals. If an individual cannot keep a mentally tight grip on the twenty to thirty things they need to do in a week, then he/she needs to utilize a things-to-do list. It will assist you in staying focused. A things-to-do list saves you time and helps you stay organized and focused on what you need to do for the day.

It always helps to write things down where you can actually observe the completion of the goal, and then scratch it off the list, so as to move on to the next goal at hand. If you are really determined, you will continue on to the next task. Creating a things-to-do list will help you move on. It will assist you by infusing you with the desire to not want to stop. Yes, I'm speaking to you! You are not reading this book for no reason. You are reading this book because you are determined to become trapped to succeed! It is important that you understand that when multitasking, you still have to be organized.

Many times people start out to finish their goals, but they find out that they have been talking to their friend too long or doing something else that diverts their attention, which causes them to not get anything done. It is very easy to forget that you were supposed to make a stop somewhere and fail to do it. If you keep your things-to-do list on you at all times and not deviate from the goals on the list, there is a greater probability/chance that you will get those things done. This includes making important phone calls, getting to appointments, and other things that demand time management. The more organized you are, the more successful you will be, and you will be on your way to becoming trapped to succeed!

HOW MANY GOALS
TO
ATTACK
AT
ONCE

*C*hapter 4

Maintaining Your Focus

Maintaining your focus is something that many people have trouble with, especially when they are doing so many different things in life. Therefore, the question is, how does one maintain his/her focus? How does one overcome this problem? How does one stay focused in a world that is constantly changing, a world where it appears as if there's never enough time to finish where you left off? One way is to never give up! Maintaining your focus is not as hard as it seems. However, one must be clever and have a ton of drive and tenacity! I, for instance, was able to keep my focus by minimizing the things around me that would distract me or throw me off focus! One major thing is the reduction of recreation. Yes, I said recreation. People will tell you that you have to have some form of recreation, and that's true, but if you study the average millionaire, they all have one thing in common: They put a lot of things on the back burner, for example, sleep, hanging out with friends all the time, watching little television, because they have their own vision.

They also minimize how much they go out for recreation. Extracurricular activities, such as movies, dinner, and other social events, have to take a back seat if you want to see your goals become a reality. People who are successful have a tremendous understanding that sometimes you simply have to say no for a while. The bottom line is you must make an action and decision to be successful. I once heard a multimillionaire on *The Oprah*

Winfrey Show state that she didn't want to be broke all her life and then further stated that she noticed that all her friends were wearing name brand shoes, jewelry, and other expensive clothes. She stated that upon noticing this fact, she thought to herself that the people who are manufacturing these things must be rich. She stated that she said to herself, "I'm going to start investing in stock, in the very things they were buying!"

My point is instead of hanging out at the mall every chance she got, she did research on investing. She did this while her friends were hanging out at the mall, shopping. While they were shopping, she was at home, investing in stock. She stated she invested in the very things that her friends were buying. My point is she kept her focus on becoming rich! Maintaining your focus is not as hard as it seems, but a person who wants to achieve a goal does take some discipline. Recreation is fun! However, being successful with your recreation is even more fun!

I personally thought that how she came up with that idea and how she was successful because of her discipline on maintaining her focus was great. Can you imagine how many times her friends called out to her and wanted her to hang out and she had to say no? I need to tell you that this young lady was an adolescent. Yes, she was not an adult.

Can you imagine the countless graduates that successfully attend college and graduate with four-year, six-year, and eight-year degrees? That takes commitment, drive, and dedication! I salute you all. It's not an easy feat! Nevertheless, the reward is worth the pain and sacrifice. All the same, a person with a positive goal and follows through and completes it deserves recognition.

I want you to imagine saying "no" right now to your friends. Imagine saying, "I have some work to do." Imagine that it is bright and sunny outside and that you yourself are seeing your friends go out of town for the weekend on a great road trip without you and you have to stay home and finish a personal project. If you cannot say "no" to recreation and fun and maintain your focus on a consistent level, more often than not, it will be very difficult and/or next to impossible to become trapped to succeed! Becoming trapped to succeed takes great commitment and unwavering discipline, wherein you must be able to focus despite the many temptations that you will face.

Yes, maintaining your focus can be difficult. It can be tough, but the pain and hardship is worth it in the end because you'll be where you want to be. Don't worry, I'm not saying you will have to cut everything out of your life, but there is a time for everything. You have to have some form of discipline to maintain your focus. You have to be diligent at completing your goals. If you can maintain your focus, before you know it, you will be where you want to be in life! You will have learned that one of the crucial elements to being trapped to succeed is the power of having a focused mind!

You will come to understand that when you make up your mind on something to do and maintain your focus, there is nothing that can stop you once you have made a realistic decision to get it done, once you have determined within yourself to not let go, to hold on, and to keep that internal focused drive, that mental focused ambition! It will take you to the top! Believe me, and this is based on experience, that when you do this once, when you taste that power of maintaining your focus and you have and understand the power of a focused mind, you will never, ever, be the same again!

You will become a great achiever, and you will never want to go back. There are many people in the world who possess that power, but even with that great amount of achievers, there are still few who understand the concept of maintaining your focus on a deeper level. It is a necessary evil to maintain your focus when everyone is pulling and tugging at you. Maintaining your focus takes a lot of strength, but you can do it! Some of us do it through prayer and belief in God, in Christ, that He will see us through. This is a very good way.

For Christ is the way, the truth, and the life! (James 14:6, KJV) It would also help if you would surround yourself with positive like-minded people to assist you in maintaining your focus and want to obtain success just as much as you do. I probably said this before, but I'll say it again, you must be mindful of those whom you allow to share your space, especially when attempting to maintain your focus. Everyone has different types of goals, and some goals are more in tune with what you are attempting to do, while others may sway you from your focus.

It is also critical to understand that one should surround himself/herself with the things that they desire, even if this means using pictures to keep their mind focused on obtaining them. If you do not submerge yourself in the things that you want to do, they can fade away to a distant and faraway dream. It is the decisions that we make that shapes our lives, and that ultimately provides us with the power to prevail over the obstacles on our journey!

The element of being focused is so powerful, so great, that when one is focused and refuses to stray from the path or straddle the fence, you will be looking at a person who is virtually unstoppable because that person will never give up! They will never stop trying! They simply will never let go! You should make up your mind that if you really want to achieve your goal, whatever goal it is, approach your goal with the attitude of never quitting and never giving up!

No matter what happens in your life, you must be committed. Sometimes you may have to pause for a minute. Sometimes there will be those moments when you will place your dreams on what appears to be a hold, but you will always remember to go back and finish what you started. You must behave as a heat seeking missile that will not lose its target. You must remember that nothing will stand in your way, not even the test of time! I encourage you to live the best life that you can and to live as fully and as full of light as you possibly can.

My mother always told me to "treat people right" and to "be kind to others." Sometimes this may be difficult, but this will help you in keeping your focus where your dreams will leave dreamland and become a positive reality!

WHAT IS AN EFFECTIVE STRATEGY AND HOW TO UTILIZE THE CONCEPT OF HAVING AN EFFECTIVE STRATEGY IN YOUR LIFE?

*C*hapter 5

The Effective Strategy

In this chapter, I will explain what an effective strategy is and what are the benefits of having an effective strategy. So let us first find out what the word *effective* means. *Effective* is defined as being able to produce a desired outcome, or result. I have used an effective strategy that I will share with you, and I can tell I was a winner every time. However, before I go any further, let us find out what the word *strategy* means. *Strategy* is defined as (1) the science of planning and directing military operations, (2) skill in managing or planning, especially by stratagems. *Stratagems* are defined as an individual's plan to defeat any enemy. In this chapter, it is my goal to expose you to another way of overcoming obstacles, another way of simply getting things done! I want to show you how to control your environment and the variables that exist within them so as to produce positive results in your life, so you will be a great achiever and not an underachiever. I now begin this journey on learning by taking you into the benefits of having an effective strategy. This way, every time you have a goal to pursue and/or an objective, something you set out to do, you will overcome its odds.

Nevertheless, you must remember that you will have to stick to the plan that you create, unless modifying it is essential, because there is minimal room for negative, unplanned deviation, unless God himself tells you so, depending on how successful you want to be or how timely you want to see results. In this chapter, I will share with you short stories and provide you with examples on what an effective strategy is as it relates to getting things done effectively. Now it can be said that there are many people who have effective strategies, but the question remains, was the strategy that they utilized effective or not? If you noticed in the above definition about strategy, it mentioned the word *military*. I can tell you this: If you are trying to achieve anything worthwhile or achieve something great, believe me when I tell you, you will be at war with your attempt to accomplish it!

Great goals are not tackled easily! For instance, I begin with this brief story about becoming a police officer. In 2001, I applied to several police departments. One gave me the opportunity to test for their agency. However, I was overweight at the time. My ideal weight should have been in the ballpark figure of 180 lbs. At the time, believe it or not, after getting married, having children, and eating my former wife's food, I gained substantial weight, wherein I weight 245 lbs., although I held it well. I was expecting a call from the police department that I had just taken the written exam with and very well understood that I was now on the clock. My strategy was to begin the workout process. I purchased a treadmill for the house along with some weights, and I was determined that I would be ready when they called me for the physical-agility portion of the test.

The physical-agility portion of the test included a mile-and-a-half run that had to be completed in 13 minutes and 46 seconds, which I could not have achieved at the time. It also included bench pressing 98 percent of the applicant's body weight, stretching the applicant's fingers so many inches past the applicant's toes, and then the applicant had to do at least thirty-seven sit-ups in less than 60 seconds. I'd heard how many people would pass the written exam but could not pass the physical exam. I was determined that this was not going to be me. I knew that the written test was the portion of the testing that I needed to get past first. My effective strategy was to ask every police officer who I came across what the test they had taken for their department was like and what it consisted of during their testing phase. I talked to officers everywhere, stores, squad cars, and everywhere I would see them. Later in this book, you will read about the importance of contacts and networking.

However, let's continue on with the story. I needed to know what types of questions were asked, how much time does an applicant normally have to take the test, and what books were *most effective* in assisting applicants in passing the test. Needless to say, I received all types of positive answers. The answers that they gave me were critical in helping me pass the test that so many others had failed. My short-term goal was to constantly get information from experienced officers. One officer informed me that Chicago State University, where I was attending at the time, had police-officer-training books. He didn't have to tell me twice. I quickly bought the book and started studying. The book was a wealth of information. It basically told me everything that I wanted to know about how to pass a police examination.

Since I enjoyed reading, my strategy was to study in the morning and in the evening. I replaced my magazine time with reading about police training. It was a tradeoff that had to be done. I was always on a road trip to go somewhere, so instead of listening to the radio, or conversing with my friends, I would read the book until we got to our destination. My other strategy that was effective was to take the book to whatever car I would be riding in. I also took the book when going shopping with people, especially a certain female family member who took all day in the store; that gave me three hours to study right there while she went in various stores and before I help with the grocery bags. Shortly thereafter, I received a call to take the written exam, which I passed. It was sad to see others receive failing grades, which is one of the reasons why I have written this book. I can tell you right now that, psychologically, my mental process on a cognitive level was that I was going to pass the test because I had studied hard enough and effectively enough! I had gained the skills needed to be successful! I was mentally prepared to succeed, and you will be too!

The physical exam was a very difficult process for me, which I would not have been successful at without having an effective strategy. I definitely needed an effective strategy to complete my mission. The reason it was so difficult is the fact that after passing every phase of the police exam, which includes the written test, the physical test, the psychological test, and other tests, they can hire you but not call you for one to two years because they are hiring other people who made it to the hiring list earlier than the new hires did. Why is this so difficult, you ask? Imagine waiting for two years to start a new job that you love and that you have already been hired for and knowing that when they call you, you will have to be ready in one week to pass another physical fitness test, which is not a problem if you are in shape. However, for individuals who are not in shape, they can forget about it.

This is where the effective strategy came into play! However, let me tell you the requirements for my age range at the time in 2001. I had to run at least a mile and a half under 13 minutes and 46 seconds, bench press 98 percent of my body weight, complete thirty-seven sit-ups in under 60 seconds, and be able to reach at least 5–7 inches past my toes without bending my knees as part of a stretch test. Now understand, when the police department calls an individual after being hired, which could be at any time, a year or two or in a moment's notice, which will more than likely be when you least expect it, you will be given one week to be sent to the police academy to take the physical-agility entrance exam. If an individual is not ready and that person fails, they will be fired from that department. In some cases, they will be given a second chance, but that's it. If the person fails again, all the testing they completed over a year or two ago will become null and void, making all that hard work that they did to get hired by the police department obsolete.

This is why I had to have an effective strategy! I wanted it bad, it was my heart's desire to serve and protect, and although I had been hired, the battle was far from over. I went from 245 lbs. to 180 lbs. Now I had to keep it off. How was I going to do that? Believe it or not, it took the police department that I was hired with approximately two years to call me for the final test to become a police officer. But because of the effective strategy, I was ready for the call—I was in tip-top shape! The effective strategy that I used for two years to stay in tip-top shape had paid off. During the nearly two-year period that I had waited, I decided that my strategy was going to be to surround myself with workout equipment. I strategically placed the treadmill in the front room where I spent a lot of my time. Every time I went into the front room, I would run on the treadmill and then lift the weights that I had placed right next to it.

I would lock myself in appointments with people who were working out, thereby forcing myself to have to work out with them. Don't get me wrong, the drive came from the commitment that I had made to myself and my friends who expected me to show up. I encouraged others around me to think health so they would not affect me negatively and I would have a positive atmosphere at all times. This effective strategy worked for me because I kept the weight off and became mentally and physically healthier. I will never forget getting that phone call in 2002. "Mr. Eric Prince, you will need to report to the Chicago Police Academy for your physical fitness exam, if you still want the job." I was mentally and physically determined to make it, and nothing—I mean nothing— was going to stop me! I had put God first! My faith was strong, and my mind, along with my body, was ready. When I went down to the police academy, I passed the physical fitness exam as if I were an Olympic athlete! I was literally ahead of everyone who was running on the track.

I had passed the test with flying colors! I couldn't believe it! I was one of the few people in a class of thirty to forty-something recruits to graduate with a physical-fitness award. I still have the physical fitness award to this day, and I continue to be active in law enforcement where I can serve my fellow brothers and sisters of the human race. To this day, I cannot get over the natural high of the success that having an effective strategy brought to my life! I thank God for my pastor and chief apostle, Dr. Y. B. Amen, who is a researcher who helped me learn and understand the fact that I needed an effective strategy! If those of you who read this book will take my advice and learn from my personal experiences and apply an effective strategy to your goals, I can guarantee that there will be a higher probability that you will have success every time, especially if you use the effective strategy correctly and it is a logical one. To this day, I am still enjoying the psychological, spiritual, financial, and mental happiness that having an effective strategy has afforded me.

I wanted to share that experience with you so that you will use some of the examples and/or learn from them, so that you can apply them to your life, on your level, for the purpose of becoming

trapped to succeed! Once you begin developing an effective strategy

in your life, half the battle is already won! Nevertheless, you will

have to stick to your effective strategy, and then you will enjoy the

beauty of success and the power of becoming trapped to succeed!

*C*hapter 6

How To Keep Your Confidence Up

Keeping your confidence up is probably one of the most challenging things to do, especially when it seems as if what you are trying to do is taking forever. However, it is extremely important to do because how can an individual remain optimistic about a goal or dream if he or she has low self-esteem or if the person is lacking confidence? *Confidence* is defined as the belief in one's own abilities, and a confident individual is sure of himself/herself. It is crucial to have the attribute of confidence when trying to become successful in your aspirations. No matter what you are trying to accomplish in life, you have to feel good about yourself, if you really want true success with your goals. I have come up with methods that will help you keep your confidence up and stay in the moment with the things you are seeking to accomplish. One method that I have learned along the way that helps me keep my confidence up is just simply *being prepared* at all times!

A person can mediate, ponder upon, or talk about whatever it is they are seeking as much as that person wants to, especially if it provides them peace, solace, motivation, confidence, and overall psychological well-being. In the field of psychology, talking with a professional psychological practitioner is called *talk therapy* (Colburn, 2013). For instance, although I am not physically in front of you, through this book, I am still positively influencing, elevating your confidence through talk therapy. In the research article titled "Endless Possibilities: Diversifying Service Options in

Private Practice," the writer states that "Mental health counselors (MHCs) in private practice may customize their work by focusing on a particular subgroup of the population, where they *choose to present issues that they are most interested and skilled in treating*, where they will identify preferred general business policies for working with clients" (Colburn, 2013, p. 198). It is also documented that practitioners may have an array of other motivating factors for broadening their horizons of the services which they offer the public (Colburn, 2013, p. 198).

In my case, although I am in the process of earning my PhD in clinical psychology, I have chosen to infuse societal members with *positive talk therapy*, which some may consider to be "positive psychology," which is a relatively new term in psychological practice that encompasses "the science and practice of improving well-being" (Lomas, 2015, p. 338). It also stated that *positive talk therapy* and/ or *positive psychology* "is increasingly recognized that well-being is not simply a matter of people's individual choices and psychological qualities, but that it is complexly determined by sociocultural factors at many different levels of scale" (Lomas, 2015, p. 344).

It is my intention, with the infusion of this book into mainstream society, to be on that scale, where many people in the human race will be able to grow, develop, and succeed in reaching their goals within their lifetime. The various methodologies and positive retrospective examples have been provided because they have a good substantial probability to stimulate the minds of those who read this book. I have created this book because of the high probability that those methods discussed can have a positive impact on societal members as "positive psychological interventions (PPIs)" as discussed by Lomas. This book was also carefully designed to purposely cause the reader to engage in various intentional positive actions that are different from that of their own so that they can become more successful in achieving their aspirations, rather than not achieving them, which can be said to be the implication of well-being science as documented by Seaford (2014).

For instance, some professional practitioners may have interests that deal with helping societal members with professional growth, the desire for more autonomy, having a sense of professional stagnation, and lastly, helping those move on with their personal lifestyle preferences according to (Colburn, 2013) as cited by (APA, 2010; Anderson & Brownlie, 2011; Browne, 2004; Carr, 2006; Hillman, 2006; Legge, 2012; Wallace, Lee, & Lee, 2010; Williams, Polster, Crizzard, Rockenbaugh, & Judge, 2003).

Therefore, it is vital to open up and discuss your goals and ambitions with the right people, like-minded people, who are trying to help you achieve your goals in life. One should commit himself/herself to spending some time discussing their goals with positive people at some point throughout the day or even the week, if at all possible, because it increases motivation and gives the person a sense of rejuvenation, revitalization, and inspiration! Doing so can also cause a person to feel stronger about their pursuits and more confident. At the same time, it can cause the person to work harder at his/her goal, which will ultimately only bring them closer to obtaining whatever it is that they are seeking after through having higher levels of confidence. Remember, the closer you get to achieving your goals, the more confident you will become! For instance, imagine learning how to walk if you haven't been able to walk in years, then all of a sudden, you are able to move one leg and then the other.

You were able to move your legs because you worked for it and kept a positive support group around you that constantly told you that you can do it! There may be people who do not necessarily need a support group because they are going to do it anyway as I discussed earlier in the book. Nevertheless, for those of us who do that, okay, because keeping your confidence up is up to you and we all have different needs. The bottom line is to get it done! Keeping your confidence up through various means that work for you is a key factor in success!

Whether it is going back to the drawing board or discussing your goals with friends, family, or peers, you will know what you need to do if you apply it to yourself and remember what worked best for you. Sometimes reading a book on something that you want to achieve can be a strong confidence booster. Sometimes people will lose confidence when they think that their goal is taking forever. Stop this way of thinking, and remember that Rome was not built in a day. Things, such as visions, goals, and dreams, take time, and they will come to pass if you apply them to yourself, keep your confidence strong, and never give up!

One of my favorite passages is Psalms 92, which states, "The righteous shall flourish like a palm tree" (KJV). If one really thinks about the context from which the Bible is speaking, a fully-grown palm tree can literally be many stories high. However, if one thinks that they will obtain large amounts of success overnight, they can forget about it. To think this way is unreasonable and will only cause the person who thinks this way great amounts of stress! Needless to say, success takes time. I have studied people who have become great success stories. If one believes everything they hear and see on television, they will believe that success occurs overnight. I can tell you that this is not the case majority of the time. *This is important to know and understand because it will assist one in being patient while they work to reach their goal at hand.* The majority of the people that one hears about being successful overnight is very far from reality or the truth of the situation. If one goes back and studies the person in question, they will discover, more often than not, that the person was trying and putting great effort in their goal to be successful for years.

Again, this is critical to understand to keep you from being discouraged along the way. You must constantly tell yourself, "I will not lose confidence in the things that I am seeking." You must tell yourself, "I am going to continue to practice, meditate, reflect, study, do research, discuss my goals with like-minded individuals who are determined to accomplish their goals as well." This will keep you determined and focused in your journey to be successful. These are a few of the elements that are necessary to keep your confidence up and that will keep you mentally and psychologically strong so that you will never give up! Does it work? Absolutely, I've done it, and others have as well. Sometimes the journey to achieving your goal can be overwhelming because of the magnitude of your dream. However, one must remember the old saying, "No pain, no gain, no fame," or maybe the one that says, "You have to pay the cost to be the boss.".

Believe me when I tell you that there is a reason why they came up with these sayings. *Any goal or dream that is worth something is going to take time, hard work, and true dedication.* There is no substitute for hard work; even if a person works smart, they will still work hard to some degree. Another way to keep your confidence up is to visualize the result. Personally speaking, I love thinking about the results and/or the way I will feel after I have accomplished a goal. Once you get hold of the feeling of being successful, you will never be the same again. The feeling of obtaining positive achievements will drive you to be more confident in yourself; your brain will be stimulated to new heights, and your spirit and soul will long for more.

Remember, keeping your confidence up means that sometimes you will have to congratulate yourself for the small victories that you have achieved along your journey. You must learn to give yourself a pat on the back from time to time, not all the time, especially when you know you're getting close to your goal because of hard work. It's okay to give yourself tiny rewards every time you accomplish a task that brings you closer to the completion of your goal.

Remember, in war, there are many battles. When you win battles from time to time, and here and there that were in the way of you accomplishing your goals, you have to take the time to celebrate small victories. Doing so helps keep you motivated and builds greater confidence. There is nothing wrong with a boost of encouragement by way of celebration from time to time, but don't go over the deep end with the reward that you give to yourself. Save the biggest and best reward for the completion of the goal—the final victory. Make a promise to yourself to do something great for having been strong and for not giving up. This will give you something to look forward to and will make you more determined to want to achieve your goal or dream.

Having confidence will take you a long way and ultimately carry a goal seeker to the top! The objective is to keep your confidence up! It takes lots of work and commitment, but you can do it! You can do anything that you put your mind to. Yes, it's a mind thing! It's all about where you want to be in life! I personally ask myself over and over, "What's your next goal?" Remember, "Without a vision, the people perish" (KJV). I had to tell myself and now I am telling you, the reader, "If it takes confidence to get where I want to be, then confidence will become a way of life for me," and therefore, it must become a way of life for you. Self-confidence is something that may not come naturally for many of us, but it is something that can be learned. Sometimes referred to as a learned behavior, confidence must be harnessed, nourished, and developed. Sometimes it may have to be discovered, which is why humans have to learn how to adapt.

In the world in which we live, it is said that "only the strong survive." In other words, the weak will fade away. It truly is a necessary requirement to have self-confidence and/or have some form of strong self-esteem. These are characteristics that are important for self-growth and self-discovery. They are attributes that should be gained in one's life to help us along the way in the obtaining ours goals and dreams and also to inspire and motivate other human beings to reach their fullest potential as well. Having confidence in oneself can help one relax in challenging or difficult situations. It also helps others who look up to those who are confident to relax in times of uncertainty when they can observe that there is a confident person among them.

Confidence gained by a person can assist in helping one to understand that no matter how long, no matter how hard, and no matter how many other people are trying to do the same thing that a person is doing, what you are doing is unique and special in your own way. The attainment of confidence assists individuals in understand that they have something no one else has and that what they have is needed in society. Confidence helps one to be sure of his, or herself. There are many people who suffer from lack of confidence. Confidence is your individual special characteristic, confidence is your insight, and confidence is a gift to yourself and other people who need it to be inspired! Therefore, work on your confidence and the skills that it takes to maintain your confidence. This raises a question: How can one be more confident? The answer is hidden in the words *preparation* and *practice*. Preparation, through practice, should be a critical element in your life if you want to be confident in the things you do, such as completing a challenging goal. Confidence is something that comes natural for some, unnatural for others, but even those who are naturally confident, they still work at being more confident with themselves.

For instance, let's look at Michael Jordan who I referenced earlier in the book. Michael Jordan was arguably the greatest player to ever play in the NBA. Although he was the greatest player, this did not stop him from working on his fundamental basketball techniques. Working on the skill sets you have will only sharpen your abilities and make you more confident. Another example that can be used is that of a singer. The more a singer takes voice lessons, the more they learn to sing. The better the singer's voice becomes, the more prone they will be to sing in front of large crowds because of increased levels of confidence. Yes, I do agree with the saying "that practice makes perfect," but what kind of practice? Practice that is *deliberate, consistent, meaningful,* and *passionate* is the kind of practice that will increase your confidence and take you where you want to go! For in doing so, you will experience life all over again, where you will have many newfound successes in life!

*C*hapter 7

Maintaining Your Pace of Determination

Determination is a necessary attribute in gaining any type

of success. Determination stems from a person's intentions to do

something (Oxford University Press, 2015). It is an individual's

purpose for wanting to achieve a goal (Oxford University Press,

2015). Determination can be described as one's firm intention and/or their unyielding desire to complete an action (Oxford University Press, 2015). The reason for this is, if an individual is to do something, more than likely, they are going to do it. A good example based on personal experiences and what I have observed from others is that people stay determined because they don't want to fail. Nevertheless, as humans, we will fail sometimes, but that does not mean a person has to stay down. You get back up, dust yourself off, and try again. This is the way humans learn to overcome the obstacles that are before them. A person can stay determined by being competitive.

A lot of my personal determination come from being competitive. Competition is a great way to stay determined. The reason for this is one has to always have a purpose or intent. For instance, if I know I am in a competition, and I know I don't enjoy losing, the understanding of the fact that I don't like to lose will give me all the more reason to stay determined to accomplish my goal. Let's say a person is in college, and they are there with their best friends whom they grew up with from the fifth grade, and they are all there with the same career goal in mind, and everyone from their community knows that they have set out to go to college and complete their degree with an expected outcome of success. This would be the factors that would or should cause motivation, that would propel each of them to complete their goal. Most people in this situation would be determined *not to go back home* without achieving their goal.

When you have competition, it ignites a whole new level of determination. Competition is a positive psychological stimulant that is useful and effective in assisting you in sustaining high levels of determination. It is important to understand that just because a person has a goal, it does not mean they will have the necessary amounts of determination to complete that goal. Determination must be maintained, and it can be exciting with competition. When used in a positive way, it can help one succeed in life.

A little healthy competition can be a positive force that can go a long way. A person can even compete with himself. For example, I would set goals, but not only would I set goals, but I would also set dates with each goal. Doing so would assist me in maintaining my determination and keep me in a competitive state of mind until I complete each goal. Remember, if you can maintain your determination, you can dictate where you want to be in life. Some of the greatest that were ever accomplished were achieved by determined human beings who would not give up! These people held on to their beliefs and were stubborn to the core. They simply would not lose their determination which pushed them to the top.

Furthermore, these people did not listen to all the nonsense and rhetoric that the unbelieving and faithless people around them were attempting to impute into their lives. In times such as this, I can tell you from my personal experiences that I have told myself, "I am going to do this, and nothing is going to stop me. If God be for me, who can be against me?" In this world, there will always be negative factors that you will have to deal with. Deal with them strategically and move on. Strong individuals who possess the qualities in this book will not lose their determination because of a few issues they have to deal with but will persist until they make it through any and all challenges. It is important to know that strength has to be taught. Strength is a learned behavior, and if a person is not strong now, they can learn how to be strong.

Humans can learn to be strong by associating themselves with strong, positive people. This is called vicarious learning and/ or learning by way of observation. This book is teaching you, the reader, to be strong by way of information, some of which comes from empirical evidence that the writer has personally lived through and some from the testimony of others. Helplessness is also a learned behavior. To stay on the track of completing a goal, we must take a position of power instead of a position of helplessness. So when we look at determination and the things we need to do to stay determined to complete our goals, the success of the goal will many times far outweigh the struggle.

Imagine what the world would be like without people being determined to get things done. There would be no skyscrapers, no airplanes, no cars, no electricity, and no phones to talk to loved ones. There would also be no entertainment, no football games, no basketball games. Needless to say, the world would be a very boring place. We as humans would literally be stuck in the Stone Age because nothing would get done. However, it is because of those people who have possessed the power of determination and a mind to not give up that we are where we are today.

It is because of the competitive drive of those individuals who are determined not to fail but to succeed that we have embarked on new discoveries that make the world not only a better place, but also a place that is more interesting and exciting to live in. Now we can observe things that we would have never seen and go places we would have never dreamed. The human mind can imagine many things, but if the human race has no passion or desire and/or no determination to obtain them, then what good would it be to have a mind of great imagination and vision? This is why God, through Christ, gave us heart and soul.

The heart and soul of man were given so that we as humans could put our visions and dreams into action by way of drive and determination. The beauty of determination is that it gives a person the desire to achieve even the most difficult tasks. If you, the reader, will take notice, you will discover that you hear the word *determination* in success statements, such as these: "the person was determined and could not be stopped" or "a determined actor came to Hollywood with$10, along with the clothes on his back, and look where he is now." Do not be confused, everyone who goes to Hollywood with only $10 and their clothes on their backs will not become a success. Those who have done so, defied astronomical odds and had some form of insight that others did not have. Nevertheless, you can believe this or not, but the one thing that they did have, out of all their other unknown attributes, was determination. When a person possesses the true spirit or element of determination, they are well on their way to success, although determination is not the only factor that plays a role in the success of the person in question. Nevertheless, it is a key ingredient that one cannot do without.

It does not matter how long it will take, a truly determined person will not give up but will keep going until they complete their goal. The person may have other things they have to learn, but the determined individual will arrive at the destination that they have set before them. Determination will carry you over many obstacles that you will face. Determination will help an individual in overcoming or getting out of any pitfalls they will encounter along their journey to be successful. It will carry them through their up and down. Determination will be there, will carry you through the mistakes and the failures, and will be your best friend, providing you with the mind-set of never giving up on what you started.

Determination is the silver lining in every cloud, especially for a person who is trying to complete a short-term or long-term goal. Know and understand that the number one competitor when attempting to do anything is oneself and that you must maintain an adequate amount of determination to see you through so that you can reach your fullest potential in life!

It is also absolutely important that I point out that determination is one of those concepts that cannot be left out of the criteria for success! If you are not determined, how will you get through the ups and downs and the journey pains that accompany those who put forth great efforts in trying to be successful? Look at Ben Carson, Donald Trump, Steve Jobs, Bill Gates, and Michael Jordan, along with others who have paved the way in being successful. It is critical to note that every single one the previously mentioned individuals started out with minimal resources, but with their confidence, hard work, dedication, and persistency, they were able to become successful, and yes, there are many others just like them.

These people provided us a glimpse of their lives, where they shared their negative and positive experiences through their personal books, autobiographies, and movies so that we could observe that the road to success is not easy all the time, and that many times, more often than not, it can be downright painful! I recall Dr. Ben Carson in the book *Think Big*, saying that a patient of his "had the worst possible prognosis." Nevertheless, the key element to the success of the client and his successful recovery was that he was outright determined to live. After years of multiple surgeries and chemo treatments to the patient's brain and brain stem, along with other complications and recurring fevers, and a slew of other problems the patient had, he simply would not give up as he was determined to live. Needless to say, the patient survived and is said to be doing "generally quite well," according to Dr. Carson (*Think Big*, 1992, pp. 127-129). This is a testament to the attribute of human determination. Never doubt a determined human being.

When you are on a mission to be successful in life, and you desire nothing less than the best possible outcome, believe me, there is going to be hardships trying to get there. It makes no difference whether or not the person is black or white. If you want the prize, you have to go through storm and fire to get there. As human beings, we must maintain the belief in ourselves and the goals we are seeking to accomplish.

I know it can be hard, I know it can be difficult, and sometimes it seems as if you are never going to reach your goal, but you will! This is where your determination must kick in. This is where you need to ask yourself, "How bad do I really want it?" This is the crossroad between success and failure, and you have to decide whether you will go on or not. You have to make up your mind whether you are going to let a storm keep you from your dream or not. I tell myself from time to time, "All right, Eric, what are you going to do? We are at that breaking point. Are you going to give up? Are you going to quit?" And my response is always the same.

"I did it before, and I can do it again." A little humor—sometimes this happens when I'm on the treadmill. As previously mentioned, taking care of the human body is essential to success as well.

I constantly check my status and reevaluate my current situation, and if need be, I go back to the drawing board. I can tell you I've been at the drawing board countless times and will be there in the future. You must understand that in situations where you know it's getting rough, and you have been at it over and over, you have to have the type of determination that no matter how many times it takes and no matter how ridiculously hard your goal seems, you will always go back to the drawing board and reorganize your plan. Remember, you are at war when it comes to obtaining your goal or dream. Nevertheless, your determination will not allow you to fail! So I say unto you, maintain your determination and stay in the fight! One day you will look up, and you will see the end of the rainbow, the rewards that the struggle you fought has in store for you! You will see that all your positive energy, sacrifice, and pain were worth it and that you have become a better person because of it.

Chapter 8

Fourteen Longitudinal, Retrospective Case Studies Based On Analytical, Descriptive, Exploratory, Phenomenological, Qualitative Research Involving Real-Life Short Stories On The Personal, Empirical Experiences That Caused My Personal Growth And Propelled Me To Become Trapped To Succeed

It is very important that I begin this chapter with transparency. It is important because people will read this book, and some of those who read this book will be in very bad and/or negative situations, and they too must know that they can and will overcome their obstacles, if they put forth their very best efforts! Some of these people will come from broken homes that are caused by various problematic situations. Some will come from impoverished communities, some from other backgrounds that have other negative environmental factors. Some will come from rich homes and upbringings of substantial wealth, and then there are some who will come from neither.

Nevertheless, all types of humans need inspiration and motivation! It is my sincere desire to reach and inspire humans from all walks of life. I myself came from a gang-riddled neighborhood and was raised by a single parent, my mother. I was a latchkey child, the eldest of five. I have four brothers and one sister. Although, these negative factors were not in my favor for being a success or for becoming trapped to succeed, something was greater in me, than that of myself, and this positive force that was in me, along with my personal desire to be the best that I could be, propelled me forward so that I could be what I am today. I believe that which was in me then is still in me today, and for that, I thank Christ, the Lord of Hosts.

Having said that, let me say this: This chapter is meant to inspire, to uplift, and to encourage people all over the globe by providing them, as the readers of this book, with personal examples from my life's journey on how I became trapped to succeed and how they can too! The empirical observations in which I experienced during my developing years will now be yours to examine and to apply to your life on whatever level that you deem best.

You will be able to learn from me and utilize my experiences from these case studies that span over two decades and took careful observations to formulate into this book. It is my sincere desire to present this book as a well-thought-out systematic package that many can learn from, which is not only based on spiritual wisdom and personal experiences, but also that of substantiated scientific evidence. This evidence correlates directly with vast discoveries that I have made about life through deep introspection of myself; from which you, the reader, can learn from the complexities of the rich phenomenon that I have provided; from which you, the reader, will gain critical insights about being successful in life and becoming trapped to succeed.

It is important to note that a rational, sound theory will be comprehensive in nature and explain various observable occurrences (phenomena) according to Friedman and Schustack (2012) as cited by Campbell (1988). In this case, my theory is that a person can become trapped to succeed in life. This is why no matter how painstakingly it was for me to write this book, I had to do it. It was painful because I wanted to publish it years ago, but the research on my observations had not been done. There were no spiritual or scientific explanations and/or substantiations for the phenomena that you now have the luxury to read about, which are derived from various peer-reviewed journal articles and various textbooks that have been selected for the writing of this book. The case studies for this book had to be exhaustive and the data had to be saturated. This means I had to be able to carefully distinguish by way of systematic observations that the same patterns of gaining success reemerged every time I behaved or executed an action in the same manner. This was the case with this theory on how one can become trapped to succeed.

What you are about to read are some of the things I did to give myself strength in my journey into becoming trapped to succeed. I learned through trial and error that success is truly a way of thinking. I learned that if I thought as a failure, then I felt like a failure. However, if I thought as one who was a success, then I felt like a success, and when I felt like a success, I started to succeed. If you, the reader, can think you are successful, then you shall be. It's all up to the one who thinks he or she can, then shall he or she be. The following experiences that you are about to read somehow stimulated my brain's neural network. Through neuroplasticity, they caused my brain to expand, made me have more intelligent, usable ideas that I thought more effectively, efficiently, and lively. This is the same as saying I became smarter, more energetic, and more self-motivated to accomplish any and all my goals that I have at present and will have in the future.

Through these empirical experiences, I observed that my brain expanded and opened up to a whole new level of creative and positive thinking. Friedman and Schustack (2012) define the term *cognitive style* as the human race's unique and individualistic way of handling tasks and solving problems. I further went on to carefully and systematically observe that the more I engaged in the things that caused me to feel good about myself in a positive way, the more things I wanted to do and the more confident I was about doing them, no matter what problematic situations arose and no matter what challenges I faced. And I have prayer to thank for this self-actualization. For without God, through Christ, I could not have made it because it was prayer that strengthened my faith. I further observed that the more I was stimulated with positive, dynamic energy, the further I went in achieving my goals. This positive energy caused me to reach higher and go further, and it was all based on the way I was thinking about the things that I was doing and the things that I wanted to do in the future. Remember, your potential to develop and improve will never stop until you cease to exist on this earth. The way you think of yourself now is where you will be in the future.

"So as a man thinketh, so is he." (KJV)

The Marshall Field & Company Experience

Case Study no. 1

In 1991, during my early college years, which began right after high school, I didn't have a lot of money like most college students. Nevertheless, this fact did not stop me from dreaming and strategically finding positive ways to obtain things that I wanted; some of which came with minimal effort, others with great effort. For example, I would always dream of having all the men's cologne that I wanted, along with nice business shirts for school. I had one good white shirt that I would wear, and I would wash it as often as needed. I would wear two pairs of slacks interchangeably with the white business shirt over and over, knowing that one day I would have many. My Marshall Field's experience was simply a grand experience just like the ceiling shown in the picture. Marshall Field's is a store that is rich in history, being built in 1852, and is also a store that has many beautiful aesthetics.

Needless to say, every time I would set foot in Marshall Field's, it made me feel, internally and externally, rich and alive! I thank God for these rich experiences. On the way to school, I would stop at Marshall Field's early in the morning and try on different men's cologne. I would do this every morning because it made me feel good, and since they would always give me free samples of men's cologne, I took advantage of the opportunity. I would think about what it would be like to have a dresser full of men's cologne to choose from. The samples that I received caused this dream to come true. Every time I went to class, some of my classmates would say, "Eric, how many different colognes do you have?" I would simply respond by saying, "I have a store full," thinking of how I would sample different colognes at Marshall Field's and how they gave me so many samples that I now had a drawer full of different kinds. These were good times, and it caused me to see things differently. In my mind, I was preparing myself for riches that were to come.

It is important to understand that it wasn't just the cologne that made me feel rich. I had discovered along the way that it was the journey to obtain the cologne that made me think and feel successful. The first element that I discovered was that I had to get up extra early to network with the men and women at Marshall Field's to get the cologne samples before class. First, this taught me more discipline and sacrifice to obtain the things that I wanted.

Second, I had to practice my communication and diplomacy skills. They gave so many samples because I was kind and showed them and their profession respect. Third, I learned during this time that people are very intuitive and that they want to be treated with respect and dignity. They want you to tell them what you want, and if they can give it to you, they will. I learned to be straightforward, humble, and patient. When I did this, the men and women of Marshall Field's welcomed me with open arms and treated me as if I were royalty, although I was a student with no money.

I learned that the way a person feels about himself/herself and the way a person treats the people around them will take you far in life and places beyond their wildest imagination. To all those workers at Marshall Field & Company, Downtown Chicago, thank you for a marvelous experience! Thank for always putting my cologne samples in nice little neat paper bags and making me feel like a million bucks! These experiences caused me to embrace people, to communicate more, and to be more open-minded. They taught me to be diplomatic, to be kind, and to embrace change. I learned all this from seeking out cologne samples from Marshall

Field & Company. Sometimes they did not have as many samples as I wanted, but this taught me to appreciate what I was given.

I learned to appreciate the little blessings that I had and to reach for the stars while I was in my period of waiting for more. I learned that the possibilities were endless and that if one appreciated the little things, then more is given. I also learned that window shopping gave me a vision of what I wanted and stimulated me in a positive way, which caused me to find a positive means to go about obtaining those things that I dreamed of having.

I realize now why my mother exposed me at a young age to people from all walks of life. She did this by not only riding numerous trains and buses to and from work for years, but also by purposefully making me speak and say "hi" to people as we rode the trains and buses to and from my school and her place of employment. It is because of this that I was more prone to talk to people and, when I got older, engage them in all types of conversations. I will have to ask my mother, but I seriously do not think at the time she understood that she was classically conditioning me to become a diplomat who would be highly skilled in the utilization of complex, positive diplomacy. Nevertheless, the intentional or unintentional repeated pairing of me with societal members would catapult me into a field that deals with the current state of affairs of mankind, which is what the field of psychology strongly affects.

This set the stage for every single experience that I would have during my high school years, college years, and beyond. For without the early exposure that was related to social interaction from all age groups and from all cultures, the Marshall Field's experience would have never been possible. The Marshall Field's experiences that I encountered were the solidification of my childhood exposure, wherein I interacted with all groups and types of people and from which the high probability of causing me to be the social person that I am today. In summary, get out more, talk to people, watch people, learn how to deal with people, and you will open up positive doors that otherwise would have never become available to you.

Books and Music

Case Study no. 2

In 1991, while in college and living with my mother, I would sit in the front room and read books while listening to music. I would literally be able to go anywhere in the world that I wanted because of reading all sorts of amazing books! Reading gave me vision and enriched my mind, while at the same time, music stimulated my soul. Nowadays, there's no excuse not to read. A person can read from a book while he/she listens to music on their headphones, or they can read from their phone or tablet while listening to music with or without headphones. I love the dual combination! The fact that one can now electronically download hundreds or even thousands of books and switch to them in a moment's notice while listening to music at the same time is a phenomenon in itself. When I read, it was as though I was cheating the fact that I didn't have a plane ticket.

The mind is so incredible and imagination so powerful that I would read a book while listening to music, and I would be halfway around the world through the details of the book. Some books are so spectacular with details that it sucks the mind into surreal experiences, and a person will not be able to register the fact that they were not there at that time in place but that they were actually reading a book. Books increase the imagination and cause greater brain stimulation, which forces more brain function to occur.

The brain is so great that sometimes I could smell the coffee that a book was describing. I would read whatever I could get my hands on. It was because of these vast readings that I noticed a change beginning in myself. I didn't notice it at the first, but little by little, I began to become more passionate about life, about wanting to do more things in life, and about how I communicated with people around me. I began to realize the more I read books and listened to relaxing music, the better I felt about myself and how I interacted with people around me. Reading made me see the things in the world as more attainable, more reachable, where I was actually not too far away from reaching goals that I had not even set out to accomplish yet. I would not only read books but also on occasion magazines that had decent storylines, for instance, *Ebony Man* magazine.

Ebony Man magazine always had little stories in it about adult life. I remember observing the models in the storylines and thought, "I can do that—I want to do that." The next thing I knew, I got the chance to call Johnson and Johnson Publications where I expressed my interest of becoming a model at the age of nineteen. They told me to come down to meet with the publishers of the magazine. So I went down to Johnson and Johnson, and the next thing I knew, I was being told that I needed an agent. I was referred to an agency by Johnson and Johnson in Chicago, Illinois, located on Michigan Avenue. It took some time, and I didn't get to model for the company right away, but I landed an audition for a billboard with Baby Ruth candy bar.

It was on the set for the shoot of the Baby Ruth billboard that I met a very nice person who referred me to the *Ebony Man* photographer, who would actually give me my first break as an *Ebony Man* magazine model. My agent said I was too young and that I needed some hair on my chest, but this did not stop me. As a matter of fact, I began my acting career with that same agent who had faith in me and who accepted me into the agency of Phoenix

Talent located in Chicago, Illinois. These are critical experiences that I would hope that you would take with you. I say this because it is very important for you to understand how reading shaped my life. No one told me to do these things.

I did them because, as a person, I had outgrown my surroundings. The reading that I was doing caused a sense of yearning and/or strong desire to do more things in life. I noticed reading also made me calmer, happier, and yet at the same time more enthusiastic about setting personal goals that I was determined to achieve. My constant reading was expanding my vocabulary; it was changing the way I thought about things and how I reacted in certain situations. There was definitely something happening to me that at the time that I could not explain the way I can now. For instance, I discovered that reading strengthens one's exposure to the world and places them in new environments, where vast things can be learned that will ultimately shape the reader for the better.

Take Robert Ludlum's Bourne series for example. If one were to read this particular series of books, it is possible that they might fall in love with languages, especially if the person enjoys an exciting spy thriller. I say this because there is a point in the book where Jason Bourne is on the phone, speaking various languages. This alone exposes one to the fact that there are humans in the world that can speak several languages. One can come to understand that if this character can speak French, German, Spanish, and other foreign languages, there is a possibility that they can do the same.

Reading increases the neurocircuitry and environmental exposure to the brain because your brain doesn't know the difference between seeing something in your mind and seeing something in the physical, which is why imagination can be very real to human beings (e.g., hallucinations and delusions). Reading can eliminate problems with conduct disorders, for instance, oppositional defiant disorders and various other conduct disorders along with depression. *Reading as a coping strategy* has been known to change people's lives. Reading has been known to stop children from making decisions that are based on negative emotionally-laden actions that could arise from being impulsive. Many of the conduct disorders that I mentioned, along with depression, are explored in the *Diagnostic and Statistical Manual of Mental Disorders* (APA, 2014).

One solution-based theoretical orientation that psychologists utilize, along with pharmacological treatments, to help with such disorders is cognitive-based therapy (CBT). It is important to know that many times, more often than not, one major aspect of CBT is getting people to read and even listen to certain types of music, which has assisted many people in becoming and being more resilient in their daily lives, which means they will be able to overcome many negative environmental and negative emotion-laden experiences that are discussed in the diathesis stress model (APA, 2014).

It is important to point out that when I was bored as a teenager, instead of going out and getting into trouble, I would read. Reading became addictive in a positive way, especially when a really exciting book was involved. I noticed that every time I read a book when I was frustrated, I felt better. Most of the time I would forget what I was frustrated about.

Try reading your favorite book when you are bored or frustrated or even angry, and you will discover that reading and being bored, reading and being frustrated, and/or reading and being angry cannot not exist for too long in the same moment. One of the two will consume the other in time, and if you submerge yourself in reading, boredom, frustration, and anger will not have a chance. I know this because I did it, time and time again, until I was able to get it down to a science. Try reading and listening to your favorite music while you wait on a very important phone call. You will notice that anxiety will disappear, if you truly get into the book that you are reading. This is important to know because different stressors can bring on physical problems.

Grab a book, avoid the stress, and have a healthier life. It sounds easy, but it takes work. Some might ask, "How I will be able to avoid stress when there are no books around?" Understand that the books you will read will enlighten you. They will help you become calmer by exposing you to vast experiences. Read positive books that will modify your behavior for the better and will cause you to want to go further in life. It is because of these kinds of books that you will want to avoid being stressed out for a happier, more fulfilling life! Therefore, you will implement your effective strategy to fight against stress, and it will work. Successful people have to know how to control their emotions, especially those who want to be trapped to succeed. Note to the reader: Go back to the *faith vision success chart.*

The faith vision success chart can be applied to any goal, vision, or dream that a person wants to carry out! Just as Sigmund Freud studied himself by way of observations and came to sound conclusions, I was able to observe patterns of success that came about through reading, where many times I listened to music simultaneously. I repeatedly noticed that there was increased stimuli in my brain which propelled me forward, time and time again, until the evidence of what was occurring within me was saturated. It was because of this discovery that I would continue to constantly engage in purposeful acts of reading and listening to music.

I noticed that every time I allowed myself to engage in positive, purposeful, meaningful reading exercises, they highly contributed to me embracing more positive thinking, intelligent decisions that manifested as intelligent, positive, thoughtful actions that contributed to my success. Based on these carefully collected empirical observations, which were derived from deductive and inductive reasoning, I was able to determine that I was becoming trapped to succeed! It was also important to conduct more than one case study on this rapidly-occurring phenomenon. This is why it is critical that the reader reads carefully and makes sure to watch for the behavioral patterns in each case study that shows evidence of success time and time again, which will lead them to becoming trapped to succeed, although there is no one definitive path.

Nevertheless, regardless of whether or not the reader watches for the successful behavioral patterns that have been demonstrated in these case studies, the behavioral patterns that directly contributed to my success will be pointed out for clarity and elimination of vagueness. As this chapter closes out, it is vital to point out that on top of the Marshall Field's experiences, which shaped me socially, the reading of books and listening to all types of music expanded my worldview. I began to appreciate words and various languages. Music taught me that all cultures appreciate beautiful music. I discovered that you could sit a Caucasian man next to a Chinese and a Hebrew man, and if one of them is reading a book that is of great influence, it will draw all their unique cultures together.

You can try this experiment for yourself. Just get a best-selling novel, and get on a bus or train with the book in your hand, where people can see the title. If you pick the right book, there is a significant probability that you just might meet a few new friends from various cultures. It the same thing with music, try playing a hit new song where others can hear it, not too loud, somewhat discreet. Play it just loud enough to allow the person next to you to hear it. You might just see them start to move with the beat, and they just might engage you in conversation.

This is because books and music are universal and know no boundaries. As I close this chapter out, it is also very important to point out that once a person falls in love with books, there is a very real chance that they may start to love all types of books. This is what happened in my personal experiences. Once this happens, the person will start to graduate to more complex books, and then before the person knows it, they are reading books on very sophisticated subject matters with no fear because books have become their friend and the mind begins to expand through neuroplasticity and starts to want more. Once this happens, a person can and possibly will discover new things about themselves that will take them down roads that lead to great adventures in their lives.

Yes, this happened to me, and it can and will happen to you, if you open your mind to reading books and inspiring music. Fall in love with books and music, and you may very well learn something so positively provoking about yourself that it will take you further than you ever dreamed! This is why I personally believe that all parents should attempt to incorporate reading time with their children. It does not have to be long and drawn out, but one would be surprised just how much fifteen-minutes-a-day reading to your children will help their brains.

I know this because in 2015, I personally observed tremendous growth with my two-year-old son, beginning at the age of one. He began to point out words, say words, and understand the difference between various animals in his picture book all before the age of two over a span of six months. He is now putting short sentences together to our amazement. Reading is progressive. Remember when you first learned to read. Now you have moved on to sophisticated and complex subject matters and various other books, e.g., spy thrillers, psychological thrillers, murder mysteries, science fictions, and school textbooks that have expanded your brain's plasticity, neurocircuitry, and overall function. This is the power of books!

Starting the Basketball Team

Case Study no. 3

When I was a freshman in high school, in 1988, I wanted to play basketball. Every year I would try out and get rejected. It seemed no matter how hard I tried, no matter how many jump shots I made, the coach would not give me the time of day. The other team members would say, "Coach! Please look at this guy! He plays ball just as good as us and can shoot jump shots very well." The coach would not give me a chance. So I joined the cross-country team and ran for the city competition, where all the schools in the city of Chicago that had a cross-country team competed in. I did this because I was told that if you run cross-country, the coach will see that you are serious about playing basketball and let you on the team. All the basketball players had to run cross-country to some degree because it helped us stay in shape and was a requirement of the coach. So I did, I came in seventeenth place in the city and qualified for state finals. The coach still did not let me on the team. If and when something similar should happen to you, do not panic! Go back to the drawing board and strategize for another way.

In retrospection, I should have left the school and gone to another school that would have given me a chance, but I didn't because of lack of mentorship. Yes, mentorship can be a very key element to success and one that can have a strong determining factor in a person being trapped to succeed. One should seek good mentorship and follow only positive advice. If a person does this, he or she will have insight about life that those who do not have a mentor do not have, that which will provide a person with a greater chance statistically of gaining higher levels of success at a faster rate with fewer mistakes. At the time, I did not have this. I never played high school basketball, with the exception of my gym period. I did not let this stop me. I worked out night and day. I practiced my skill sets, and I constantly improved.

When I left high school in 1991, I enrolled in Phillips Business College, which was a private college with no basketball team. I thought the only way to play college basketball was that you had to play high school basketball. I had always dreamed of going to college and playing for a basketball team. I checked with the school's representatives, and they informed me that they did not have a basketball team.

This did not stop me. I was motivated, determined, focused, and goal-oriented! I decided to ask them to start one. I did not know who to go to, so I talked to counselors, professors, the dean, and anyone else who would listen to me. Someone out of the bunch told me that there was an admission counselor working for the school who once played for a Division 1 college basketball team. They gave me his name, and I took him out to lunch, and we discussed the possibilities. He observed the fire in my eyes. I was diplomatic, professional, serious, and willing to listen to what he had to say to make this dream of mine happen. I could not believe that I had come this far and that it was possibly going to happen.

I was only nineteen years old at the time, but recall and/or revisit the earlier chapter where I stated that I always came dressed to school. I did not talk average or dress average. Upon meeting me, I believe the former coach noticed this and, therefore, took me very seriously. I had no idea how the meeting was going to turn out. We left the meeting with him telling me that this was going to take a lot of his time. Later that week, I received a call from the admissions counselor, stating that he did not mind helping me start the basketball team and that he would be the coach. That was amazing to my ears! I could not believe it was actually happening. He instructed me to construct a blank list with numbers and signature lines and make a list that there was going to be basketball tryouts the coming weekend.

At the end of the day, I went to retrieve the list from the network center. It was completely full and running over, where people made more lines for additional signatures. I could not believe how many people, including myself, came to try out for the first basketball team of Phillips College. It was almost overwhelming, especially since I had to try out too. Needless to say, my hard work and dedication to the game paid off. I tried out for the team, and not only made the team, but I also became the first captain of Phillips College's basketball team, where we competed with Robert Morris and other colleges in the area. The school has closed since then. Robert Morris has gone on to become a Division 1 contender in the NCAA basketball tournaments.

If I had not learned to communicate with people and speak with confidence, this would have not happened, or the chances would have been very small or next to none. If I had not tried or took the risk of possibly failing, it would not have happened. I do not think that I will ever forget the games, the gyms, the lights, the pep talks, the practices, the losses, or the wins! It is very critical to understand that one must take risks in life. For without positive risks, there can be no great accomplishments! This experience catapulted me to go on to do other greater things.

Starting and playing on the basketball team was an awe-inspiring experience! It came with many long nights, hard work, and sacrifice, but it is not one that I would trade for the world. Do not underestimate the time and energy that people put into their accomplishments. You will see their glory, but you may never know the story of pain and sacrifice that it took for them to arrive at their destinations. However, if you are willing to work hard, work smart, work constantly, work efficiently, and work effectively until your vision comes true, it will happen in time. It will take time, but you will experience emotions that you would never have thought your body would feel in your lifetime! It is my desire that you too will have many times in your life when you will feel positive, super amazing emotions from working hard to accomplish your goals and observing them come to pass.

You can do whatever it is that you want to do in this world, if you believe in yourself and put your heart, soul, and mind into it. The empirical evidence is overwhelming. We can observe many great examples from people who have been successful and who have come from situations where almost every odd was against them. People who were exposed to many dynamic challenges that were before them, which were many times astronomical in nature. Nevertheless, due to human resilience and will power, along with determination they were able to beat the odds that stood before them. Understand this: With hard work and dedication, so can you!

Dressing for Future Success and Socializing at the Water Tower in Downtown Chicago

Case Study no. 4

It was 1993, I would constantly travel back and forth to school on the bus through Downtown Chicago, taking the scenic route on Michigan Avenue. I would get excited about the possibilities of the future because of how aesthetically beautiful Downtown Chicago is. I would also get excited about being rich and going to other beautiful places in the world! Sometimes, after school, I would dress up in a nice outfit and go to Downtown Chicago, to the Water Tower, with friends and family. We would window shop as if we were rich! I started doing it by myself a lot. I would go to the best stores and envision buying the most expensive things. When the store representatives noticed me doing this, they would come to assist me, and I would simply reply, saying, "Not today, sir, I'm just simply looking so that I can determine what I want for later."

Observing people and interacting with people while window shopping, time and time again, greatly motivated me and caused me to work harder for what I wanted in my future. I would do this anytime and every time I got inspired. I observed within myself that doing this kept things in perspective for me. Mingling and interacting with people through window shopping or just by having a cup of coffee with diverse groups of people at a coffee shop exposed me to meeting so many people different kinds of people that it caused me to grow socially. I observed things during this time in my life, without understanding at the time, that some people are of the diseased personality type (Friedman & Schustack, 2012). Those humans who are of the diseased personality type have negative behavioral patterns and are more than likely to discourage you on your journey or they cannot be happy for you. I then learned about those who are of the self-healing personality type (Friedman & Schustack, 2012). Those people of the self-healing personality type have positive behavioral patterns, are resilient, and are more than likely going to encourage you to do better, while they do better for themselves as well (Friedman & Schustack, 2012). I would encourage you to connect with the self-healing type on your journeys.

It truly made me understand the dynamics of how people think on various levels, and it robustly contributed to me being a human being who would later become a humanitarian with strong humanistic and existentialistic personality trait patterns, which basically means I appreciate people on a spiritual level and care for the well-being of others (Friedman & Schustack, 2012). This type of social growth and development is vital for strong social relationships. Needless to say, this is why early social exposure for children can lead to very powerful learning experiences that will assist them in their lives later.

I would later discover through my many experiences that I was an interactionist, meaning that I now understand that people are all different and that they are all experiencing different situations simultaneously (Friedman & Schustack, 2012). Understanding this fact taught me to be more empathetic toward others, along with their situations and circumstances. Understanding this came later in life. I believe that this is why to this day I constantly give to the poor and do not view them as beggars but rather as humans who need different types of assistance for the negative situations they are in.

Window shopping, observing people, and socializing with the human race made me more determined to one day be able to walk into a store and be able to buy whatever I wanted because of hard work and dedication. It is good to have a vision of where you want to be in life. Had it not been for those visions and those moments that I had in the past; I can truly say that I would not be where I am today. Window shopping and observing the wealthy made me want to succeed even more, but I did not want to succeed without helping others.

Window shopping, for me, was and still is nothing more than a positive neurological stimulant to have a reason to go further in life and to be able to do more things for myself and others. I have since moved on to destination shopping, meaning I now pick places in the world that I want to go to and then work toward that goal! I learned that the more motivated I was, the further I went in life. The further I went, the more I was able to help, not only myself, but also others. The greatest gift in life is the gift of being able to give to others, especially those who are in need. All this came about because of window shopping and interacting socially with others at the Water Tower and other beautiful places that inspired me to do great things. My word to you, the reader: get out, get inspired, and get moving!

God Can Dream a Dream
for You Better Than You
Can Dream for Yourself

Case Study no. 5

In 2001, I was an audience member on a very popular talk show. I had come on the show with a mission. My mission was to ask the talk show host if I could be in another movie with her. The first movie I had done with her in it was called *There Are No Children Here*. I was a background actor at the time, and yes, I did get some screen time in the television show. My first thought as I sat in the audience was to tell her I did the TV show and then tell her that I am still pursuing my career as an actor and then ask her if maybe she would help me. As the talk show hosts walked out, I was pumping my fist hard in the air, doing the "dog pound thing." I was trying hard to get her attention, and I did. It actually worked! I was nervous, but it was a positive risk that I had to take. The talk show host said, "Someone is really charged up today," and the audience, along with myself, went wild. She came toward me, and we exchanged dialogue.

I told her that I was hoping that she would give me a break in film and that I was an aspiring actor. She stopped, looked at me, and the audience got completely quite, and then she asked me,

"How old are you?" I told her my age at the time. She looked at me as if her mind were racing for the appropriate thing to say to me. She then said, "Aww, you're just a baby, the best actors don't get started until they're in their thirties." She then went on to say that "If you are really serious about acting, you will move to New York or Los Angeles and wait tables—that's how the best actors get started."

At the time, I thought to myself, "Wait tables—is she serious? Move to New York or LA to wait tables!" At the time, I did not realize that doing so builds character, discipline, and would have shown me how bad I really want to accomplish my goal. After she spoke the words to me, she then turned and walked away as she headed to the other side of her audience, but then something strange happened. She stopped suddenly in her tracks then slowly turned back toward me and said these exact words, "God can dream a dream for you, better than you can dream for yourself!"

Then she turned back around and kept walking as if she never missed a beat. I knew at the time that divine intervention had taken place and that something miraculous had happened! I knew that she was right; I could feel her words beginning to take a hold of me with a knowing that God was in charge of my life as long as I allowed Him to be. I knew that I had to listen and that along my journey, I needed to put God first so that He could order my steps. Let me, therefore, say this to you: Allow God to order your steps, and He will! If I were your counselor, and you, the reader, were my client who believed in faith-based psychological practices and/or psychologists who utilize faith-based theoretical orientations in counseling sessions, I would say the same thing to you, if you were worried about your future. I would say it, and I would mean it with everything in me.

We as humans who believe in God should let go and let God! We should stop trying to do everything ourselves, when there is clear evidence that God is saying, "Okay, you have done enough. Let Me take it from here." Remember He does have to show us that He is God. How else would we know that He actually exists?

I must tell you that the words "God can dream a dream for you, better than you can dream for yourself" never left me. To make a long story short, some months later, I packed my bags, quit my job, sold my home, and off to Los Angeles I went. Understand this: No part of this story/case study is false or fabricated, even the most unbelievable parts are true, and it is important that everything written is documented truthfully as mandated by the American Psychological Association (2010), which strives for ethics in research in their detailed code of conduct. Having explained this, I will continue with the story. After only four weeks of being in Los Angeles, I had two agents, one in Santa Monica and one in Hollywood. The Hollywood agent was a theatrical agent, and the Santa Monica agent was a commercial agent. I had won $10,000 on the *Price Is Right*, was taking pictures with Jay Leno in the former green seat that he used to have on his show, and was auditioning within the month.

My pastor, Ame Sarah Amen, had later come out to visit me in Los Angeles. Upon her arrival, I determined to show her around and see to it that she had a great time, which she did. I knew, by her coming out, that something special was going to happen. As we drove through Beverly Hills, we observed signs going up. It was the premiere of the Antoine Fisher screening. I wanted to attend this event because I wanted to network and meet people whom I thought could assist me in my career as an actor. It was a tough decision, but frantically, I asked my pastor if it was okay if they left me in Downtown LA and came back and picked me up later. Needless to say, I met a lot of mega stars, and my networking skills paid off because if nothing else, I had a fantastic time walking and laughing with the stars before and after the events.

I do not ask for autographs because I am a celebrity too. Moving forward, the premiere ended, so I left and called my ride to come and pick me up. While I was waiting across the street from the venue, I had to go to the men's room, so I searched for a restroom and found one at the Baja Fresh, which was right across the street from where the premiere was and where I was waiting for my ride home. As I proceeded to the restroom, there was an inspiration poster on the wall. I looked up to read it because I am very fond of inspirational posters. As I looked up, there was the name of the talk show hosts who had wrote the inspirational phrase. It was the same phrase that she had spoken to me: "God can dream a dream for you, better than you can dream for yourself," and I must say it was a dream come true because I had met Denzel Washington who was and is the distant acting mentor that I had never met up until that day at the premiere. Because I had listened to the talk show host and left my hometown of Chicago, I experienced something awe-inspiring! And I will never forget the poster that confirmed that "God can dream a dream for you, better than you can dream for yourself."

The Drive to California: Understanding My Limitations

Case Study no. 6

In the summer of 2002, I, along with my wife and children, had finally finished packing a twenty-foot truck. I was exhausted and tired because the night before the drive, we were up all night, trying to make sure that everything was right with the house, that it was fully cleaned, and that we did not leave any valuables behind. Whether it was or not, I was determined not to put the drive off another day. It was mentally and physically draining because we had already driven to California to get one of the cars there first. We had to come back to get the truck, the furniture, and the other car, which would be pulled in the back of the Penske moving truck. I was determined to get there no matter how tired I was and no matter how long it took. I was determined that nothing was going to stop me. After all, how bad could it be? It was only a nice drive to California, right? I also did not want to put the load of driving on my wife, knowing that the truck was twenty feet long with a car attached to the back. It knew it was going to be a long haul. I drove for at least twelve hours at a time, with a few breaks in between, and persisted while everyone slept in the truck when they became tired of looking out the window. It had to be God who touched my body.

I could not have done it without Him. The ride was very uncomfortable because it was a moving truck. To make matters worse, while we were driving through Phoenix, Arizona, the air conditioning went out on the truck, and we had to drive through extremely intense heat. I knew that something had to be done, and that I could not, in good conscious keep driving to get through the trip faster the way I had originally planned. We were sweating, and we were all getting hotter and hotter. As much as I wanted to keep going, I had to understand my limitations. The human body can only take so much, sometimes just as I did. You will have to regroup or regather yourself to go farther. I searched for and found a Penske provider who would fix the air conditioner. Until we found the service station that would fix the air condition, we sprinkled cold water on the children so they would stay cool. I pulled over more times than I wanted, but it was for the good of all of us. I knew it would take me longer to reach California, but again, one must understand their limitations and always put safety first.

External problems began to arise. There was a major detour in effect that would cause me to have to drive longer hours. I realized I was not going to make it to California when I wanted to. I began to understand very well during that trip that I was very human and that I was limited in physical power. It is important that you, the reader, understand that you are limited as a human and that understanding your limitations is the very thing that may see you through difficult times.

You must understand that you can only do so much as a human being and that sometimes you need to stop and think and take precautions. This is the difference between the wise and the unwise. Many people would live longer if they would adhere to these truths. I would not have gotten to California any faster driving while being tired or sleepy. Sometimes we as humans have to step back and understand that now may very well not be the time. We must understand that there will be another day. We must understand that although risk may be a positive attribute on some occasions, in other times, risk may actually be deadly. Driving while not being able to keep your eyes open because of fatigue is the same as driving drunk. In law enforcement, the term is "felony ignorant" if one does not know or understand this concept. In other words, pull over and live to see another day. This concept can be used in many other ways. Because of understanding my limitations and pulling over to rest from time to time, we were able to make to California in one piece.

There are a lot of dangerous twists and turns and mountains to drive through when going to California, and the roads that lead to the beautiful state can be unforgiving. It is wise to study one's journey ahead to gain solid data before making the journey. Many people think just because they are going to a nice place, they will not run into any adverse situations. This is what the average person considers to be common-sense thinking. This is erroneous thinking, which will and can cause serious problems. One must utilize heuristic thinking, which is thinking that involves self-educating techniques that will lead to discovery from investigations. At the time, I did not execute this type of thinking. Had I done so, I would have known that there was a detour, which would have saved me hours and hours of extra driving. I would have already known where the nearest service station was for Penske in case of an emergency because I would have already mapped it out, which would have saved me a lot of time and energy because of knowledge gained before the road trip. What you should take from this case study is that you should *understand your limitations* and prepare for the unknown, or anything that may come up, along the way, with not just utilizing common sense but rather heuristic thinking, which is critical in the process of being trapped to succeed!

My Time in Hollywood: The Struggles and the Victories, Along with the Experiences That Provided Me with Critical Life Lessons

Case Study no. 7

The year 2002 was my first year in Hollywood as an actor who was a Taft Hartley which is a person who is given 30 days to join the Screen Actors Guild, and cannot work any further until they do so. I had not joined the Screen Actors Guild (SAG) yet, but would do so, in the near future. Things started happening fast, but not as fast as I had hoped they would for. I had been on several auditions, and I was highly successful in getting the roles, but there was a problem. One of them was when I auditioned to portray Denzel Washington in a television show that was going to be called *Facing Fame.* I arrived to the place of the audition, I auditioned, and they loved me. I went through all the callbacks, went to meetings and auditions all over the Los Angeles County area! I then waited for the phone call, but the producers did not call. I called them, and they told me that they were sorry, but the budget fell through. They further told me that if and when they do the show, they would still want to employ me. Trust me, this hurts, when you sacrifice and do everything you can to get a role and then land a role and then the budget falls through. It seemed as if this was the story of my life!

I literally landed role after role after role, with multiple casting agencies and production companies, but the budgets would simply fall through, or a company was not in compliance with the Screen Actors Guild, which I later joined so that I could get the big roles. Yes, this was very frustrating and heartbreaking! When what appears to be constant, and repeated failure is happening to a person, it can cause serious self-esteem issues. I was going on multiple auditions in a day, with multiple casting directors. They would say things such as "The man's got talent, but this is not the role for him" or "We would love to hire you, but we owe someone else a favor." I auditioned for many movies and television shows and kept receiving invites to keep auditioning. Now this is where things started to turn. I started to land television shows, film them, and they would air on television. One of which was *Wednesday Afternoon* that was filmed in 2004 by the American Film Institute (AFI), which went on to win an Academy Award in the short film division. It was a student project that was picked up by Showtime in 2004. I was able to get the role because I turned in two headshots to AFI after listening to my SAG orientation representative and auditioning for the role.

She explained that if I and/or others went to AFI and turned in two headshots, we could get more experience working on student films and taking acting classes. I did what I was told, and I did it very quickly! I started taking acting classes through AFI SAG Conservatory program and began auditioning for more acting roles. The next thing I knew, I was on the top of a parking garage in Downtown Los Angeles in the district of Chinatown. We wrapped on the short film *Wednesday Afternoon*, and before I knew it, I along with the cast were being showcased every other day on Showtime and in other outlets. Then the word came in—we have been nominated for an Academy Award in the student film division, and yes, we won! It was the most amazing feeling and had brought a sense of accomplishment. It had been two solid years since I had been in Hollywood, and it was not easy, to say the least. It seemed to be much longer.

I had been repeatedly turned down for roles that I really wanted, and the rejection was putting a beating on me, but it was starting to pay off. I was in constant traffic! Yes, evil, god-awful traffic most of the time when I went on auditions. The negative variables that were against me seemed to weigh heavily upon me during this time. Nevertheless, because of my love for acting, I persisted through. If one looks in retrospect, I had been auditioning for roles for two years before actually filming anything and seeing it appear on the screen where I was actually speaking. I bring this point up because it is critical to understand that there will be other victories along the way.

These victories are important because they keep you going; for instance, getting an agent, making my photography appointments, paying for headshots, getting in the leading man's Hollywood book that agents look at for new leading men in Hollywood. While I was not actually working on film, I was successfully building my acting career on the business side. *This took time, and it is still taking time! I still have not given up!*

You, the reader, must not give up either! "Rome was not built in a day!"

I am still acting, and I will never stop because maybe, if I get enough celebrity status, and just maybe when I become a mega star,

I will be able to save some child who would not otherwise listen to me when I tell him or her that I am not only an actor, but that I am also a doctor, a writer, and an educator, among other things, and that no matter how hard life is, they can and will overcome if they never give up. I will tell them that if they keep trying, if they keep being determined, if they keep putting their little hearts and souls into their goals, dreams, visions, and those aspirations that they truly believe in, they will succeed! From my experiences, I realized that things take time and that patience—true patience—is a virtue. I realized that if I continue to take care of myself, I can stay young and still look good on screen. Yes, I said it—still look good on screen where I will give the world a Denzel performance because I love my job as an actor.

If I truly believe in myself and in acting, and if it is not all about me but others, then I cannot allow myself to give up. We as humans must keep ourselves motivated and determined to accomplish those things we believe in. Why can't I be a doctor, an actor, and a writer among other things? Why can't I be super successful with the goal of helping others? This is my ultimate goal, and yes, it does not come easy, and it will not come easy for you all the time either. You must do everything in your power to not allow yourself to lose focus or get knocked off your hypothetical or theoretical square. You must fight for what you believe in. You must be constantly in your pursuit of self-improvement, self-development, self-evolution so as to be effective in being able to help others to do the same. I have had many failures, many ups and downs, through my experiences in Hollywood and life in general, but it has taught me to be strong and to be persistent, to be flexible, just as Bruce Lee said in an old behind-the-scenes video, "You must be like water," and where he said, "If you pour water in a cup, it takes on the form of the cup," among other descriptions that he made about water being flexible.

Even now, in 2016, I have discovered that if I am going to make it into acting on the level that I want to make it in, I must be flexible to auditioning dates, filming dates, and table read meetings. I must be flexible and ready, but at the same time, producers and production companies will have to work with me as well. Yes, sometimes you have to draw the line and let them know what you will and will not do. You must keep your soul pure if you want to be the best you. There are many things that will come to challenge who you are, but you must remain steadfast to survive in this world. You will be challenged! I auditioned for shows, such as *In the Line of Fire, 10-8, Everybody Hates Chris*, among other television shows and films where I did not get the roles but came very close, which was very frustrating. After some time, I sat next to great actors and thought to myself, "What is he doing here?" I would say to myself, "Wait a minute, that's so and so from that major television show."

I auditioned for big-budget movies and did not get the roles, but I was liked by the producers, and they kept calling me back, but it was not without strong competition. What my agents and managers did not tell me was that once Hollywood starts to recognize you, you start going on different types of auditions. What I mean by different types of auditions is that I would be sitting next to well-known stars, but they were stars that were still auditioning for roles. Just because you are a star in Hollywood does not make you are a mega star who does not have to audition for roles, namely Denzel Washington, Will Smith, Julia Roberts, and John Cusack, among others. I learned that an actor could become a celebrity who has significant celebrity status, but *without* a household name and no significant riches.

I had to discover this reality for myself. I began to notice that they did not need me to audition a small fraction of the time because they would call my agent and say, "Can you please have Eric read the script and see if he wants to portray the character in the movie?" which were small costarring roles, not huge multimillion-dollar roles. At least not yet. I still did not realize that I was becoming known in Hollywood's circle of producers. My persistency and dedication to the craft was paying off. Suddenly, in 2007, something happened. Yes, after five years of extremely working hard, auditioning, and scrapping for roles, something started to unfold very quickly before my eyes, and it almost seemed to be happening in one day.

My manager Johnny Pena sent me on an audition with a major studio—Warner Bros. I went to the audition for the major studio, and as always, there was a ton of people sitting in the hallway, waiting to audition for the role of an LAPD bomb officer for the television show *Studio 60 on the Sunset Strip*. There were many people in the lobby waiting to audition, and then there were those who had already auditioned for the role but were leaving. There were so many guys auditioning that it was almost impossible to avoid anxiety and/or the feeling of being defeated. Nevertheless, I must tell you I was able to avoid those negative feelings, and I will tell you why.

I was prepared, and I felt good about myself, and I was looking good because I had cut my own hair and gave myself a nice fade (haircut). I was super confident, and when I walked into the audition, I owned it! All those years of auditioning had paid off. I became a seasoned auditioner, and I became an actor that is ready for the camera. I walked in, spoke the lines, and before I could get home, they were already calling my agent, saying, "We want Eriq F. Prince, and he does not have to come in for a second audition. He's got the role!" This was my first time working for a major studio. At this time, I was living at least an hour outside of Los Angeles and/or Hollywood. I got home and was in the living room area a few hours after the audition. I heard a knock at the door. I opened the door, and there was no one there, but there was a script in a neatly-sealed package at the door. I took the script and went back in house. A few hours later, in the late evening, there was another knock at the door. The studio had sent another script with revisions, but no one was at the door when I went to answer it. It was very mysterious. I cannot explain the adrenaline, the emotions of joy and happiness that I was feeling. It seemed as if everything that I was working for had paid off in one day, but I knew this was not the case. I had worked very hard for this, and it was beginning to pay off.

It is important that you, the reader, understand that this did not happen overnight. It is critical that you understand that no matter how much technology advances in the modern world, no matter how much faster things seem to be, there are still some things that take time. Therefore, on a side note, let me encourage any and all medical doctors, MDs, that will read this book, you can and will make it through your residencies. However, you must understand that it is going to take time and that there is no room for social media during your residency training. Social media must be kept to a minimum or completely shut down during some aspects of your clinical rotations and/or intense study periods. Social media will distract you.

You cannot afford to fall behind and not complete your residency training because of depression.

The medical field has increased in data, and things are not the same as when other MDs went through school. You must understand that your learning experiences will be much more intense than ever before because of the many medical advancements that have been made. If you stick to your plan, you will make it through, but there will not be time for too much else other than studying, which will be your life. Choose your extracurricular activities carefully, but do celebrate your victories and then get back to studying, forsaking all other distractions. If you do this, you will avoid depression and have a happier, more fulfilling experience as you become a medical doctor.

To get back to the case study at hand, I started learning my script that night. Warner Bros. told my agent that they agreed to make me a costar on the show, which is what my agent negotiated.

This would be my first costarring role on NBC during primetime. *Studio 60 on the Sunset Strip* starred Matthew Perry, D. L. Hughley, and Amanda Pete. I was very happy and appreciative to be among them.

I arrived at Warner Bros. Studio and drove through the massive gates. I parked my car and asked for directions on where to go next. I observed a line of people checking in and asked was I supposed to be in that line too. The security guard asked me for my ID. I gave him my state ID and my SAG card, and he looked me straight in the eye and said, "No, Mr. Prince, you need to meet with a producer, they will have to take you to your trailer." It is important for me to convey to you that there are emotions in this world that you will feel that you have never felt before, which will be greater than any drug you can ever experience. If you work hard, work smart, and do not give up on yourself, you will get where you want to be, and you to will feel these wonderful awe-inspiring emotions too!

I remember the first time I made it on the International Movie Data Base (IMDB), it was a very good feeling to know that I was being recognized to some degree for something that I love to do. This was a feeling of great success and still is a feeling of success to this day because I still can be seen on the IMDB, http://www.imdb. com/name/nm0697648/, where my career in acting continues to flourish. It is small achievements such as this that gave me emotions that have left me and that will leave you standing there frozen in time, where all you can do is ask yourself, "Is this really happening to me?" My desire is that you, the reader, will be wise, be strong, and never give up in the pursuit of your dreams! Yes, the pursuit of your dreams will be difficult for many days, and pursuing your goals will feel as if they are taking long and that the pain sometimes will be unbearable.

However, if you can stay the course, you will make it, and you will experience some of the most surreal emotions that you have ever felt. You will be successful, and you will never stop being successful because you will have experienced the all true fact that persistency, dedication, along with the ability to focus, and have positive relentless work habits will pay off!

This is my gift to you. All things are possible in time. Be patient with yourself and others, and you will eventually get there with persistency, unwavering faith, and God seeing you through. Remember, God is all powerful, and He will be there for those who seek Him, but He is not an excuse for lack of hard work and dedication. You as a human being, along with your personality, will have to grow and become redefined many times, where you will learn to encompass, and inhabit many new complex biological, environmental, and social changes to get where you want to be. As humans who are constantly evolving and changing, we must learn how to adapt and become new creatures in our life's journey. Human beings develop and evolve and therefore, cannot stay the same. They are expected to go to new heights and new levels. Human growth and change is inevitable, and without it, one will remain stagnant and unsuccessful.

Every living thing is growing and evolving. This is key aspect of human evolution, growth, development, and success! A successful person will constantly learn new things and reinvent themselves with the world around them; not for the negative, but for the positive. They will adapt no matter how difficult the situation at hand may seem, no matter how painful it seems to be, whether they want to or not. To be successful, I had to understand that change was inevitable, and for that to go further, I had to be resilient in nature with the understanding that I was going to have to be redefined over and over and over again. This is what I did to get where I am; this is what you will do too. This is what you will do to get where you want to be. If you know you want a specific job, but the only place that is hiring for that job is in another state, you will have to move to that other state, or you will not get that job. I have done this, and because of it, I have gained valuable experiences, and those experiences that I have gained have taught me very critical and valuable life lessons. The world has become less intimidating because now I know that if I have to pick up and go, it's just something that I have to do.

The contemplation process is much faster. I learned this all from my pursuits of becoming an actor in Hollywood. The talk show host was right! "God can dream a dream for you, better than you can dream for yourself.". Had I not moved to California; I would have never experienced any of these dynamic life lessons. You, as the reader, must broaden your horizons and be wise in doing so. There is a world out there that is waiting for you. This does not mean be hasty, be unwise, go unprepared, but sometimes we as humans have to be flexible and ready in a moment's notice. This is why we should be somewhat prepared for the unexpected, sudden, positive changes in our life.

The Screenplay and Book
That I Did Not Think I
Could Write until I Tried

Case Study no. 8

Sometimes if you want something done, you are going to have to get it done yourself! Therefore, as humans, we must elevate our minds! We must step out on faith and believe we can overcome the many odds that we are faced with. One's mind and brain really is a terrible thing to waste. The brain, which powers the mind, is a very powerful instrument that can learn anything if given the opportunity. Scientists are still putting forth rigorous effort to discover new insight about the brain. The brain is fascinating! It can expand and grow quickly. Neuroplasticity is very real. Do not underestimate the power of your brain to adapt, change, and reach heights that you never dreamed of. The only person limiting you is yourself. Stop limiting yourself and reach higher! You will be surprised at how amazingly brilliant you really are. This case study begins in 2003, when I was actively seeking someone to help me write a screenplay for an idea for a movie that I had come up with, which was an awe-inspiring script. I knew that I had come up with a major-motion-picture idea, which was and is going to be a blockbuster at the movies, although I will have to modify the title to some degree. That's another part of this case study that I will save for later. To get back to the story, I was not a writer, or at least I did not think I could be. I could not see myself for one second writing a screenplay. I let fear deter me from trying it first.

I could not see myself writing a screenplay, or anything for that matter, but this was about to change. I started asking different people how to go about writing. I interviewed various people where I had in-depth conversations with them about writing. The data that I gained was intense. I was told that there was a lot involved with screenplays and that there were many technicalities involved. During this time, I was working, going to school, plus auditioning, and it was a lot of stress. The last thing I needed to do was place the burden upon me of trying to tap into an unchartered territory, which I was clearly not exposed to. Nevertheless, I persisted because I felt as if all the good action movies were being given away.

I wanted to do action films, I wanted to do big movies, but it was not going to be as easy as I thought. I had to do something, and I had to do it quickly was my mind frame. Therefore, I continued to talk to and interview people at length, having very long discussions which turned into seminars, where I would ask these professionals how I should go about writing. One director told me to doodle. I asked, "What is doodling?" He told me that "Doodling is when you just write your thoughts down on paper." He said that "You will be surprised with what you come up with." I spoke to a mail room worker for a large talent agency, and he told me that he would help me by sending me old scripts, along with printed blogs about writing, and to read them over and over until I figured it out. As ordered, I did just that.

I continued to read and study numerous articles and blogs on writing, and I learned a great deal. Many of the screenplays and articles on writing, I still have in my possession to this day.

As I began to gain more knowledge about being a writer, and my brain started to expand with data, I began to gain more and more confidence. I noticed that my thoughts were exciting! They were riveting! They were dramatic and intense! I had something on my hands. I had discovered that I was limiting myself and that it was time for me to begin the journey of writing a screenplay that would shock the world. I was still not prepared to write alone, so I sought out a couple of people to write the screenplay along with me. I sought out writers from AFI, who told me that they would assist me in writing the screenplay. It took me few times to learn that if people do not do what they say, then you will have to move on. I learned that if you do not get a phone call, and you are the only one making the calls for help, and you do not hear anything in return, then it is time for you, as an individual, to move on. Do not let others limit you because they do not believe or want to assist you in your vision. I did exactly that—I moved on.

As I continued to write more and more, the better I became. I started by writing treatments, which are normally one to ten pages in length and which provide critical information about the story that one is trying to convey. The next thing I knew, I was looking at a full-length screenplay that was very fascinating and intriguing to read. I took the screenplay to AFI and asked them to assist me with a table read, and they told me they would look into it, to put it kindly. The writers who I originally asked for help eventually heard about the screenplay and wanted to be a part of it, but it was too late. This is not a reflection of everyone at AFI as an institution, and many of those who are affiliated with AFI contributed greatly to my growth and development as an actor and as a person. I will always be grateful for the great times and many learning experiences that I gained from the institution.

As I developed my screenplay over the course of a year and a half, I eventually published it with the Writers Guild to protect the title and the contents of the screenplay. I learned from this process that there were many screenplays that had been stolen in Hollywood, so there were really no guarantees that it would not get out that I had written a screenplay and what it was about. This frightened me to do something I never would thought I would do. It propelled me into another level of writing. I then turned the screenplay into a book. It took me two solid years of gathering the data for the screenplay and then writing the screenplay and the book. It was as long process because I wanted to write something that was sophisticated and captivating! Hence, the book *Agent 008: The Untold Story: Operation Earthquake Tsunami* was born. Many people enjoyed the book, and to this day, I am still in the process of working on getting the movie made.

This was a major learning experience, because I was not knowledgeable about the fact that when you do a spin-off, or sequel to an existing work of literature, the way I did, one must ask, seek, and obtain permission. It is important that one understands that this was a critical error on my end, and it is an error that I will never forget. I inadvertently utilized one of their concepts, the double 0s, from the 007 series, in writing a screenplay and book, and I apologize to the James Bond 007 franchise for not knowing, or understanding this out of pure ignorance. This is why the movie will not be called "Agent 008: The Untold Story" but rather another title, so as not to unfairly present competition to the James Bond 007 franchise. Needless to say, this will not happen again. This is one of the most critical aspects of this particular case study that I want to share with the readers of this book.

Moving forward, the gratification that came from pushing myself to move forward and to begin a writing career as a spy novelist was very rewarding. It was rewarding because I discovered that the only person who was limiting me from writing was myself. I learned that fear and anxiety were holding me back and that if I wanted to be successful, I had to learn how to eliminate fear. I learned that one can eliminate fear by doing research and understanding the forces that they are up against. I learned from this process that things take time, that if I put forth the effort and really applied to myself the things I learned from what others taught me, then I too could be a success.

This was one of the most rewarding times of my life! All this came about because I was determined not to be bound, not to be limited! I thought it was too hard to do at the beginning and that maybe I was just the type not to write screenplays or books. I discovered that I was wrong and that I could do anything that I put my mind to. I told myself that I will never, ever, doubt myself again, and you shouldn't either! It was through great perseverance, dedication, and willingness to learn that I was able to accomplish my goal of writing a motion picture, which has now been turned into a book which people have read and enjoyed, and to this day, those people are waiting for the sequel to come. I will not let them down. The sequel is forthcoming, along with a trilogy. It will take hard work and sacrifice, and I thank Ian Fleming for being a trailblazer for myself and others. If you ever want to know the pain and sacrifice it takes to come up with a spy thriller, go and watch the autobiography of Ian Fleming. It is truly a fascinating story.

I had to make many sacrifices during the writing of my book to get it finished, just the way I am sacrificing now to get this book finished. I listened very carefully to a person on TED Talks say some people will never accomplish great things because they gave up on their great talents and dreams for social activity. I must say he was right. Everyone is not going to resist that movie, that dinner outing, or that lunch with friends to sit in a room by themselves to strain their brains and lose sleep, sex, and other extracurricular activities that mean a lot to them to accomplish great things. The social activities shall be their reward. This is the difference between those who will become trapped to succeed and those who will not. I am not saying that one should not have some form of life, but one must understand that to achieve great things, social activity and extracurricular activities will be limited to a substantial degree.

I discovered from this experience that God has given humans/mankind one of the most powerful instruments on earth. That instrument is the human brain. Without it, we could do nothing. This is why neuroscientists and clinical psychologists, along with other types of practitioners, actively seek ways to advance the human brain. The National Institute of Health (NIH) constantly financially supports research that seeks to advance the human brain through rigorous and robust scientific studies and scientific experimentations that will ultimately assist mankind's life. (National Institute of Mental Health, 2015). God gave us a brain to do great things with; it is up to mankind to figure out how to use it effectively and efficiently with minimum waste.

We as humans must understand that if we actively seek growth, development, and evolution, there is no limit as to what we can do.

In retrospect, had I not sought to learn and grow and evolve as a writer, there is a great possibility that I would have never reached this level where I now have a deeper understanding of myself and that of other human beings. I now understand that we are here on this earth to help others, just as those who helped me. One of the major things that we exist to do as humans is to share the knowledge that we have gained. This will cause people to apply to themselves the knowledge that they have gained from others so they can go further in life, for better futures for themselves and others in the world in which we live.

The Matrix Experience

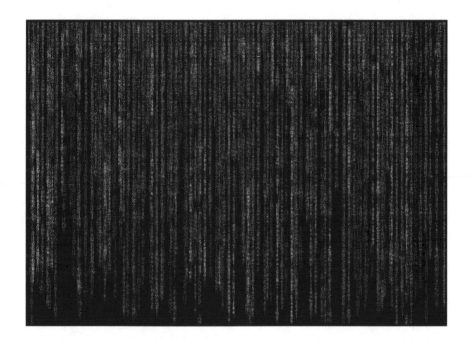

Case Study no. 9

The motion picture *The Matrix* had a very dramatic effect on my life. I was affected deeply and had a surreal experience after watching the film. It is highly probable that the movie affected me because I was going through a lot of obstacles in my life around the time I went to see the movie, and this is a major aspect of what the movie was about, in my opinion—overcoming obstacles. The scene that affected me deeply was when Neo, who was portrayed by Keanu Reeves, finally understood near the end of the movie that he had the power to overcome the forces against him. The movie inspired me to believe that I could overcome anything if I would only free my mind.

At the time, I did not understand that the movie/film *The Matrix* had awakened me and propelled me into a subconscious "cognitive shock" of metaphysics, quantum physics, probability amplitudes, positive forced oscillations, space and time, cause and effect, and the power to resonate deeply within myself; all these scientific concepts were documented by Albert Einstein, Isaac Newton, and other credible scientists. I will not go into the concepts mentioned because if I did, this book would come in more than three volumes. These concepts are very deep, and they correlate with my deep-rooted belief that God caused something to occur within me and then the world around me. These scientific concepts subsequently led me right back to the dynamic understanding that positive thinking and positive visions will result in robust levels of positive vibrations that truly matter in the pursuit of one's goals and dreams if one wants to be consistently successful. I further learned from these scientific concepts, which I believe have been shared by God through Christ, that the projection of one's vibrations, whether negative or positive, will manifest at a later time.

This is why it is critical to diligently watch one's thinking patterns because they do emit waves into the world which will have a direct effect on the person doing so at a later time, where sometimes later may be the very near future. As humans, we are a part of the cosmos; we can release darkness or light from our inner selves which will again manifest in one way or another. There is truth to the aspect of cosmology and human light transference on future things not currently seen as possible truths, along with the possible future existence of one's thoughts manifesting physically into the environment which will, without controversy, come from the mind. Think on this: We are human beings, and I have discovered for myself that as human beings, we are part of the physical universe considered as part of the totality of phenomena in time and space, which means we are partly made up of not only energy, but also that of light within the spectrum of the universe.

According to Einstein, energy is neither created nor destroyed but only transferred (see Einstein's theory of relativity). This means whatever energy we as humans release into the atmosphere, be it good or bad, it must go somewhere. Energy is not something that is powerless. It will do cause some type of effect or consequence to occur whether we observe it or not. I am now, to a great degree, cognizant of what it means to be "cognitively shocked." It is important to note that these concepts are very real and have been scientifically tested by Albert Einstein and other great scientists.

In 2001, I was pursuing a career with an agency that was very difficult to become a part of because of having over a thousand candidates. Not only was there over a thousand candidates, but the testing process was also a very grueling and long drawn-out process. This may sound strange, but if one studies the above-mentioned concepts, he or she will come to some degree of understanding about what I am going to discuss next.

I wanted this job very much. I went down to the location that I wanted to work for and had someone drop me off. I went into the establishment and was getting ready to come back out with an invisible check in my hand, as if I had worked there already and had received my first paycheck. Upon getting ready to come back out, I stopped to utilize the restroom. On the way out of the restroom, I observed a person who worked at the facility. I told him I was getting ready to test in the near future with the agency and was hoping he would give me some training in advance. He agreed and showed me a few things that I would be doing, which was very humble and kind of him. Thanks, Rich! You know who you are. Needless to say, I left very, very excited about what had occurred! Once I left, I told the person who had dropped me off what had happened, and neither one of us could really understand the magnitude of what was taking place.

Nevertheless, having someone train me in advance was very important to me at the time, but I only knew how this positive decision would impact me on a minimal level because I had released a robust amount of positive energy and light into the atmosphere, and it was sure to physically manifest soon. I threw strong vibrations off on a parallel level within the unseen universe, and these positive vibrations were soon to come to fruition in the observable future. Locard's theory of exchange just got deeper. Yes, we always leave something that can be traced back to us as humans. What about our internal energy which we push outward from within? What about the light or darkness that we purposely exude that can be traced back to us? Is it being traced back to us to some degree, form, or fashion? I say yes. Have you ever been to a person's house and when you left, you felt warm on the inside because of a nice experience with that person? You could trace that energy back to that person. This is why we stay with people we feel good around because, as humans, we can trace positive energy back to its source, and we want to be around that source of positive energy.

I had not experienced "conscious cognitive shock" at the time, only "subconscious cognitive shock." Furthermore, this was something that I had to do to prove to God that one of the positions was for me. The department that I wanted to work for only had eight positions open but had over a thousand candidates applying for the jobs listed. This did not matter to me; I had made my claim mentally, physically, and spiritually and had thrown out every positive vibration that I could think of on that establishment. I even drove around the building playing Brian McKnight's "Win" seven times, releasing positive vibrations into the air while praying. I was also inspired by the biblical story of the wall of Jericho, found in Joshua 6. This took away much of the stress and anxiety that I was feeling about the process and gave me newfound hope. I also prepared for the test intensely through various practice tests and asking critical questions about taking that kind of test. I refused to let anything stand in my way, not even myself.

After a year of testing, thinking positive, seeing myself working at the establishment, visualizing being in uniform, forcing positive vibrations into the air, along with going through various rigorous processes, I got the call, and started work. I now know that "So as a person thinks, so is he or she" (KJV). The movie *The Matrix* and the story of the wall of Jericho still inspire me to this day. We as humans must step outside our way of thinking which we consider to be normal. We must free our minds to the possibilities of infinite new heights and depths that come from spiritual and scientific levels of knowledge that will catapult us into positive levels of exponential growth and success!

It is my strong belief that there is a high probability that the things that I did were critical components in me gaining employment with the agency. To this day, I still practice the above-mentioned strategies. I see what I want, and I visualize it, I think on it, I push positive vibrations into the air and stimulate the environment in which I want to be a part of with my presence and with God's presence within me. This comes right back to what can be said to be a new element of faith-based therapy in psychological practice. We as humans have to have something positive to hold on to.

Eric F. Prince

Having belief in something can have robust potential in destroying the feeling of hopelessness, anxiety, and stress. It is my hypothesis and working theory that "faith without works is dead" as described in the book of James, KJV. In my life, I have observed what faith with works have done for me and what freeing my mind to new knowledge can do, whether it is spiritual knowledge, scientific knowledge, or both. Having said all this, my message is clear: Free and open your mind to higher heights and deeper depths of knowledge and wisdom which will broaden your horizons and expand the way you do things. The more you act on these positive things, the greater, stronger, and deeper your "human agency" will continue to propel you forward.

How I became a Contestant on *The Price Is Right* with Bob Barker

Case Study no. 10

February 2002, I, along with three others, had purposefully come to Hollywood, California, to be on *The Price Is Right* because we wanted to win money, which we needed, and a car. So off we went to CBS, where I learned from interviewing various sources in depth that you can get on the show as an audience member and have a chance of being picked to be on the show if you could get to the gate first, stay all night, and get the no. 1 ticket. Those individuals whom I talked to said get there early. I listened very carefully to these instructions, but I did not know how early they meant. I was told to get there about 2:00 a.m., but I asked myself, "If this person is saying be there at 2:00 a.m., I wonder how much earlier do I actually need to be there?" I, along with three others, arrived at the gate of the studio at approximately 10:00 p.m., just to be sure to get a spot at the gate. I understood very well that that the CBS studios did not open the gates for the line until approximately 9:00 a.m. the next day. Nevertheless, I found a parking spot right in front of the gate, got out of the car, and as I was walking up, I could not believe that there were people sleeping about five feet from the gate.

Someone came out of the tent to speak with me because they were trying to stay warm as it was extremely cold that night. I told the person as they made their claim of being the first person there that they would have to stand at the gate all night to be no. 1. The person looked at me in disbelief that I was willing to stand in front of the gate overnight in the blistering cold to get the no. 1 ticket. I did not bluff. All through the night, wind ravished me. I could only think to myself, "I did not know that Hollywood got that cold at night." All through the night, as I stood there at the gate, the three people in the tent kept unzipping the tent and peeking out at me to see if I left.

Needless to say, I did not budge because I knew what the result was going to be. This is the first lesson you should learn about this case study: If you absolutely know what the result is going to be for your goal or that there is a high probability that what you are seeking is going to happen, you must remain constant, consistent, and unmovable in the pursuit of your goal. If not, you will not reach your goal, or it will take much longer to achieve than you want it to. Goals are meant to be reached. I say to the readers of this book, "Be constant, be diligent in the pursuits of your goals and dreams."

Sometimes you will face what appears to be overwhelming odds, but you must remember, only the strongest and the wisest will survive. This is why, as I was freezing, I had one of the people I was with bring me a child's jacket out of the car. It was big enough to put on, but anyone who observed me in it knew that there was a grown man with a child's jacket on standing in front of CBS studios, refusing to leave the gate to go home and change. This is where adaptability comes into play. This is where the strongest resistance becomes a key factor. This is where confidence, determination, faith, focus, motivation, inner strength become very real, especially when I could have said, "I'm done, and I'm going home to my warm bed and a hot cup of coffee to drink."

Yes! Believe me when I tell you, "It got real!" I had come this far, and I was not turning around. I knew that if I had given up, I would never wait in line like that again to be on a talk show. It had to be now! Finally, as the night tormented and ravished me with cold slashes of wind, I could see a friend of mine peeking over the horizon. It was the sun. It was the most beautiful thing I had ever seen at that moment. It came with warmth, and it was very generous with its heat. Finally, the time to open the gate came around, and when I observed how long the line was, I was very pleased with myself, and so was the crowd that cheered me on. There were news reporters and a line around the block.

There were hundreds of people standing behind me, but I was so fixed on making it through the night that I planted my face against the lock of the gate and kind of fell asleep standing up and never noticed how long the line had actually grew. I was shocked to see the length of the line the next day. There were so many people, only a quarter of the line was actually able to get tickets. The line literally stretched around the corner, which was approximately two blocks long. Anybody who has ever waited in that line knows that the blocks surrounding CBS are very long.

As I continued to wait in front of the gate patiently, but cold and tired, a security officer walked up and unlocked the gate. I recall the look on the security officer's face, asking me if I was I the first person at the gate. It was noisy, and people were screaming and waving at me, and I waived back excitedly while answering the officer, saying, "Yes, I am the no. 1 person, and I've been here all night".

The officer then asked me, "What time did you get here?"

I replied, "I arrived here at approximately 10:00 p.m."

The officer was approached by the people in the tent who tried to make a case for the no. 1 spot. The officer then told them that to get the no. 1 ticket, they should have been at the gate and not sleeping in a tent away from the gate. The tent people were kind and congratulated me after their confirmation that they would have to be nos. 2, 3, 4. The secret to being absolutely called up to the panel by Bob Barker was that you had to be no. 1 at the gate.

As time passed, and those who were in line had been escorted to the window to retrieve their tickets to be on the show, I was approached by a representative of the Bob Barker show who took me aside and, with an honorable look, said, "So you got the no. 1 ticket on the show, huh? Follow me."

As I was being ushered down a back way onto the studio lot, I felt this surreal rush of positive emotions. This is why successful people do not quit! They do not give up! The negative of staying in the cold was worth the positive gain of the experience that I was then partaking in. As we walked through the back way, I could hear the studio audience members screaming loudly! I was let in through a backdoor and strategically placed in the front row. The next thing I knew, Bob Barker was calling my name. I could not believe it was happening to me, but it was, and it was happening fast.

I heard those famous words from Bob Barker: "Eric Prince! Come on down!" I jumped out my seat and went up to the panel. I played the "match the price to the item" game to get on the show. Upon guessing the price, Bob Barker, with his own words, said, "Eric, for the first time in history on *The Price is Right*, you guessed the exact amount of the items right down to the dollar and cents."

I went on to win $10,000 in cash and prizes. My family and friends could not believe it. It was the faith and works that I put into it to win, which inspired others to have more faith as well. My point is that when you hold a strong belief in a goal, dream, or vision, go after it. Sometimes you may not have the most perfect plan in place, and sometimes there will be difficulties along the way that will require you to make sacrifices.

Nevertheless, if those of you who truly believe in your goal, dream, or vision are willing to be committed to that thing which you believe in, you will become a success, and you will win, and you will inspire others to do the same. Reaching goals take time, discipline, hard work, and patience, but if you truly believe in yourself, you will make it to the top, and you will be ravished by the desire to embody that same feeling of gratification again.

This is why those who have tasted success and victory keep coming back for more and more of these awe-inspiring experiences!

Know that you too can be successful. Know that there is light at the end of the tunnel. I can relate to you and tell you firsthand that sometimes it does not feel that way. Sometimes it may feel as if your goal or vision is not worth all the extra sacrifices and energy that you are putting into it, but I am here to let you know that it is. I said it once, and I will say it again, if great success was easy, everyone would be a great success! A person has to make up in his or her mind how successful they want to be. For instance, everyone who reads this book will not become trapped to succeed. The fact of the matter is there are a few of you out there who will read this book and apply the concepts that I have laid out for you. I have poured my heart and soul into this book, and yes, it was very time-consuming, but I believe in you.

I believe that you are reading this book because you are looking for answers that have not been given. I believe you are reading this book because you are looking for a different way of doing things. You are looking for new facts, new data, new knowledge, which will ultimately bring about a new understanding within you. I believe that somewhere deep down in your mind, soul, and spirit, something is going to click by the end of this book. You may have to read it more than once. You will definitely have to reflect and meditate on this book. You also will need to take notes because this book gives you a sort of blueprint on becoming trapped to succeed.

This book provides you with multiple systematic concepts of being successful; some of which are methodical, calculating, and that takes great human confidence. I believe this is what you were looking for, and you found it here. I built you a bridge, and now you can crossover to the other side. It is important for me to understand the current state of affairs as a budding psychologist. Many people read self-help books. This self-help book had to be different in nature, scope, and context. It had to do something different, and I truly hope I have achieved that goal.

It was and is important that I truly believe in positive social change and that I was writing a book that would take the readers' mind to another level of thinking. This is why I discussed metacognition earlier. Understanding metacognition is just that powerful. I will not go into metacognition again, but even that concept alone has a high percentage of elevating one's mind, if one will truly grasp the concept and understand it as a general idea that can be applied to their lives for growth and development.

This is what I went through during my many learning experiences, especially the case study that you are getting ready to read next.

Anderson and Brownlie (2011) discuss some very critical points about emotions and talk therapy and key aspects of everyday lives in their journal article. One of the things that stuck out to me was the title that they came up with, which is "Build It and They Will Come." This is what I was doing. I wanted to construct or build a book that was so effective and dynamic, it could relate to the majority of the general public; a book that when people read it, they could find not just one or two concepts that relate to them, but multiple concepts that could directly change their lives for the better, whether they are young or old, boy or girl. This is why the title "Build It and They Will Come" by Anderson and Brownlie affected me the way it did.

However, the authors had more than just a great title. They believe in talk therapy, but they also believe in what the public thinks about talk therapy. This prompted me to have to think outside of the box when it comes to talk therapy as it related to success and obstacles and how I could integrate talk therapy into a book. It was important to make it fun and exciting while simultaneously being transparent, so that others could observe that even successful people go through things. And that we too have our moments just as I did when I was waiting in line to be on *The Price Is Right* and when I was beginning a career as an actor in Hollywood. It is important to understand that you will go through things, but if you can endure the pain and suffering, you will be where you want to be in life.

Comedy on the Sunset Strip at The Comedy Store: Laughter versus Stress

Case Study no. 11

There was no way someone could have ever told me or convinced me when I was in Chicago that I would have ever done comedy, especially at the Comedy Store in LA. I would have never thought in a million years that I would be doing comedy at the Comedy Store on the famous Sunset Strip, where comedians, such as Eddie Murphy, Robin Williams, Martin Lawrence, Richard Pryor, Andrew Dice Clay, and many more, performed. It was not my goal to be a comedian. It was not because I couldn't be funny, but because I only could see myself as a serious dramatic actor for the silver screen and serious studio networks, such as TNT, NBC, and CBS, among other serious networks that dealt primarily with dramas. I had just moved to LA, and I was still looking for work when a friend of mine said, "Eric, you need to go to the Comedy Store and get on stage."

I thought to myself, "I do not do comedy. Why is he even telling me about the Comedy Store?" I was told that Whoopi Goldberg and other very serious actors did comedy and that they would do impersonations at the Comedy Store. I thought about for a second or two, then said to myself, "Look at where Whoopi Goldberg is now. How could I not give it a try when others, such as Whoopi Goldberg, had done comedy and then went on to be very successful actors?" I decided to take my friend's advice and give comedy a try. I went down to the Comedy Store soon thereafter. Upon my arrival, I discovered that you had to get there early in the morning to sign a list. The list was designed for the first twenty people who got there. I would pull a number, and then whatever number I received out of twenty numbers, that would be the number that I would appear on stage. No one wanted to go first! The best numbers to get would be 7 through 15 because the comedian got to go up in front a nice crowd of people, not too early and not too late. Once a comedian received his or her number early that morning, they were instructed to come back by seven o'clock that evening.

I would go home and write and make up jokes that were directly affecting me at the time that were based on real experiences. I would talk about what I was going through as an actor in Hollywood and things of that nature. My jokes were always clean but real. I did not know that I was going to get the overwhelming response that I did at the time. I had a great command presence on stage, and the audience laughed every time I went up. I had a few comedians tell me that I was going to get my own television show. The crowd thought I was hilarious, and all I was talking about was my life experiences. Many people thought I was a natural, which may have been because of my theater training. The more I went on stage, the better and better I got. I began to pick up momentum, and people started to notice me, which is why I landed several acting roles from being referred by other comedians.

I think one of the best things that I learned was what other comedians go through along their journeys to become successful. They have a very rough job, and I commend them for what they do. I learned that Jay Leno was on the road for over twenty years before he received his big break. Not only did he suffer greatly along the way to get where he is at, but other comedians, Kevin Hart and Mike Epps to name a few, did too.

What I learned from doing comedy and what you can learn too is that humans should not take themselves too seriously and that they should learn to laugh at the little things. Being a comedian taught me to relax more in front of people, and just because one does not work in a particular field, that does not mean they shouldn't give it a try. Comedy is definitely a form of therapy because a comedian gets to talk about themselves on stage and make people laugh while doing so. It's a win-win situation. It definitely taught me not to take myself too seriously all the time.

I learned from my comedic experiences that sometimes in life, when we are seeking success, we will face very difficult challenges and go through many tough situations, but that sometimes it's okay to shed a tear and keep moving. However, sometimes we can laugh at them as well. I learned from the same comedic experiences, not to just to try one avenue to reach my goal, but to try many. I say unto you, the reader, you too can learn to laugh and self-heal. Comedy is truly a great way to incorporate laughter into your life as a form of psychotherapy.

We all need to laugh from time to time. Studies show that the more we laugh, the more we release toxins that can cause harmful diseases. Laughter is good for the mind, soul, and body. Laugh a little! Laughing got me through so many difficult times in Hollywood. Even though we were all struggling together, just getting out, being around others, and discussing our problems, our ups and downs, helped a great deal.

Laughter really changed my life, and it can change yours too! Successful people have to have a way to release tension just as any normal person under pressure does. Try laughing away your stress, it can have a very powerful effect on your life.

M&M's:
Discipline and Patience

Case Study no. 12

One of the most humbling experiences of my life was when I had to sell M&M's to make a living in 2005. It truly taught me discipline and patience. Selling M&M's for a living taught me that no matter what, there is money out there to be made. You're probably wondering what I was doing selling M&M's to make a living instead of working a regular nine-to-five. Let me explain. It's like this: When I was going on auditions during the day, it was hard for me to hold on to a regular job.

I did everything I could, including working the graveyard shift. Nevertheless, this got in the way with auditions as well because if someone did not show up in the morning, I would have to cover for them on the day shift. If I attempted to leave early, the supervisor would be short for workers, and it would have been less than honorable to leave without someone to cover a post. Therefore, I would stay and work and make auditions when I could.

This presented a major dilemma for me as a person who was doing all he could to pursue acting at the time. I could not keep allowing myself to miss out on major roles because of not being able to make auditions. I began to think deeply about a way out. At the time the only solution that I could think of was what could I do that would allow me to set my own schedule, make money, and provide for my family.

I was going through hard times, trying to make money as an actor, but my passion for the field would not let me give up or quit. I decided to go to a store that sold M&M's in bulk and buy a box or two so that I could make a small profit. I would buy a box or two and sell a pack of M&M's for a dollar. I also learned to have more respect for people who sold things, such as the Girl Scouts and other vendors who sold candy. It did not matter whether it was in a school or in front of a store. Because I had to sell candy to keep my schedule flexible, I grew to have a strong appreciation for those who sold candy to raise money for fundraisers and for those who just needed to raise money for whatever reason.

I never looked down on people who sold candy, but after I had to sell candy, it definitely caused me to see that selling candy is an artwork and that it takes discipline and patience to do that kind of work. I sold peanut M&M's because it seemed that, statistically speaking, there was a higher ratio of people who preferred peanut M&M's to those who preferred plain M&M's. I would make enough to pay the rent and other bills. You would be surprised how much candy profits can add up.

I would literally dress up in business attire to sell the candy. I presented with a very professional appearance as if I worked at a law firm. I kept the M&M's in the freezer and sold them cold on hot summer days. People loved when I sold cold M&M's! I would go everywhere to sell them. I greeted people with a smile and professionalism. Some days where better than others, but I always made a profit of some sort.

I learned that if you are trying to make an honest living, people are willing to help you. Some people would ask me, "Why are you selling M&M's?" And I would tell them straight out, "I am selling M&M's to make a living," and they would say, "Ohhhh, okay, I guess that's good enough reason as any." Yes, I had one person actually say that. I had other people ask me for permits. I had to leave from some locations and go to other locations that would actually allow me to sell M&M's on their property without a problem. Some people would ask, "Why are you dressed up?" And I would say, "Because I am a professional, and this is my job." Some people would give me money just because I told them the truth. It was very fulfilling, being able to make my own schedule, but it was very challenging as well. Selling M&M's taught me to not be biased to a great degree. I learned that the very people whom I thought would not support me supported me. I remember hearing a story about Brad Pitt being in a chicken costume on Sunset Boulevard before he became famous.

I didn't want to wear the chicken costume, so I sold the M&M's instead. Not that there is anything wrong with wearing a chicken costume to make money. Remember, as you read earlier, one must be willing to adapt to any situation that will be for their positive growth and development. Selling M&M's made realize who I was as a person and that I was only becoming stronger and more confident in my capabilities in dealing with obstacles that presented themselves in my life. It taught me that sometimes we as humans will have to be patient with ourselves and do things that we may not necessarily want to do, but it will be a positive force in our lives. I also learned that you have to humble yourself to be exalted (KJV). I truly believe that God used M&M's to teach me to appreciate success and to never forget where I came from. I would have never thought that God would utilize candy that melts in a person's mouth to keep me grounded as a human being.

M&M's made me appreciate life on a whole new level. It made me appreciate the big jobs and being successful. I recall being on set for the TV show *Studio 60 on the Sunset Strip* and making sure to treat all the background actors with dignity and respect because although I was in a costarring role with celebrities like Matthew Perry and Amanda Pete, it was one of my first major roles on film and that I still had a long way to go. Little life lessons like this can make a person or break them. I can say with confidence that selling M&M's have contributed to the man that I am today. I am sharing these stories with you, readers, because someone will read this case study, and they too will one day sell M&M's, and those M&M's may very well feed a hungry family or keep someone from being put outdoors. I am very thankful for my M&M's experiences.

The Police Academy

Case Study no. 13

I can truly say that one of the toughest situations that I personally have ever been put in was the road to graduating from the police academy in Chicago, Illinois, in 2000. I must say that the men and women whom I served with in law enforcement and others from all over the world had to overcome a great feat to become police officers who serve and protect citizens. Those of us who made it through encountered no small amount of pain and sacrifice to assist others in some of their darkest hours. To make it through the academy, it takes a special person who has high levels of endurance and resistance to pain.

One must be resilient on all levels. If those of us who went through the academy could not endure pain or difficult moments, we would never had become officers who could serve and protect. I will write on this briefly, as it does relate strongly to this book. I learned a great and many things from my experiences in the police academy. I learned that although I had a great instructor, who was very kind and professional, it did not mean he was not going to be hard on us as cadets. What it did mean, however, is that when you care for those you are teaching, you will be hard on them to maximize their fullest potential.

This is something every human being can learn whether in a police academy or not because you will go through the academy of life. On a constant basis, as a cadet in the Chicago Police Academy Metro Division, I was challenged in many different ways. I had to learn to become adaptive and resilient. Life in general is no different. One cannot fold under pressure because of the obstacles and challenges that life will throw them. What God is attempting to do is to allow you to overcome various situations so that you will learn how to bounce back from hardships. Those who cannot bounce back will give up and will succumb to the hardships of life, as my pastor would eloquently say, but with brutal honesty, he would say that to his congregation to get us to thicken our skin for the negative encounters that we will experience in life.

In the police academy, a cadet's day starts early. I would have to get up at 4:30 a.m. to get to the academy to start my day at 6:00 a.m. If a cadet is late more than three times without a strong valid reason, they would be dismissed from the Chicago Police

Academy. This is where discipline, sacrifice, and hard work come into play. This is where a cadet has to count up the cost. On a personal level, I had to rethink everything I was doing with my life as far as extracurricular activities, the way I was eating, the way I was drinking, my state of mind, and my state of being. Sometimes in life, when a person is trying to pursue a dream, they must understand that they will have to give up some things to gain other things.

There were many days and nights when I wanted to go out and hang out with family and friends. However, I knew if I did this, I would not meet the demanding requirements of the police academy, and I was determined to protect and serve. Therefore, because this is a case study, the question remains—what are you determined to do? And what are you willing to give up to get there? If you, the reader, will recall, there were *twelve cognitive behavioral questions* that were asked earlier. These questions were asked for good reasons, and they are questions that one should constantly ask oneself when making a decision to accomplish a goal.

I gave up a great deal to become a law enforcement officer, and I do not have one complaint. It was some of the greatest moments of my life. Serving and protecting is quite liberating. This is why many great men and women do it, although it can very well cost them their lives. The badge stands for something, and the cadets have to go through a great deal to obtain it. If an individual wants something that has value, it usually will not come easy. For months, I personally watched family and friends leave me, to go and have a good time during the spring and summer, while I sat at home behind a desk studying law.

This was very painful, but it had to be done so that I could complete my goal. For months, I had to leave family and friends at various places where we were all having a good time because I had to get up early. If I did not maintain a strong sense of discipline and separate myself from those good times, I would have not completed my goals. One must understand that humans have to devote their lives to hard work and sacrifice because, if one does not, no matter how many times one attempts to complete their goals, they will fail, if they are not disciplined as a person who believes in hard work and sacrifice.

This is what separates superior human beings from non-superior human beings to a great degree. Let me also say this: Do not complain when going through these stages in life. Complaining only lowers your internal motivation and drive! If one must complain, do not senselessly complain because this is just time wasted and time that turns positive energy into negative energy. While in the police academy, I knew that no one was going to tell me to get up in the morning or to go workout or to study the law or to be on time. It is the same way in life and when attempting to accomplish your goals. As a matter of fact, one may just very well experience the opposite. I will tell you this: Before entering the police academy, I went from 245 lbs. to 170 lbs.

I lost the weight because I wanted to be healthier. I wanted to feel good about myself. It did not come easy, but I did it and kept the weight off. In this life in which we live, we as humans have to make up our minds about the things that we want. As humans, we must be realistic about our goals, or we will waste valuable time when we may as very well have done something else. I say unto you this day, do not waste your time! Take care of your business!

Count up the cost for what you are trying to achieve and make a sound plan on how you are going to go about achieving your goals and dreams. Know and understand that they will not come easy all the time, but there is a high probability that one will have to have discipline and hard work to reach their goal, which will not come without sacrifice as well. Yes, you will feel the pain. Yes, you will suffer. Yes, you will go through the anguish of being alone many days. But as you go through these hardships, you will begin to reach your goals, and as you begin to reach your goals, you will discover that it was all worth it.

One will discover that everything that they thought they were missing will still be there. I discovered that I was personally glad that I missed some of those things because I was able to hear the stories of the things that I missed. I discovered that people respected me more for going through the hardships, where some even told me that they wished they had my discipline and hard work ethics. Hearing these types of words of encouragement made me even stronger.

I grew from these experiences subsequently and discovered that all the pain of being socially isolated for those brief moments in time was worth it down the road. Human beings who want to exceed average levels of success must learn that sometimes it will take psychological resilience of the mind to get to where they want to be. I have discovered that if one can be psychologically resilient, then physical resilience will come, hence the term "mind over matter." In conclusion, I learned a great deal from my experiences from the Chicago Police Academy and would not trade it for the world. It is my goal that other human beings will learn from my experiences as they too go through "the academy of life."

Chapter 9

Not What You Know, But Who You Know: The Importance Of Contacts And Networking

Case Study no. 14

In this chapter, I will explain just how serious it is to get out and network; how important it is to be social, especially if you're in a field that thrives on connections. I'm a people person; therefore, to some degree, it is easy for me to network and make contacts that lead to vital relationships in many of my career goals. On a daily basis, I talk to people. I know many people who say, "I'm not the type of person to go up and talk to people or the type of person to just strike up a conversation." Unfortunately, these are the people who would not be as successful because of the fact that they will not open their mouths and talk. It is critical to note that we as human beings do not have to talk to everyone. However, it is very important that when there is an opportunity present that will directly affect what a person is doing in their career choice, then this may be the time to open your mouth and speak up.

It is very critical that you apply this chapter to your life as I have discovered that without networking, one can only go so far in their endeavors. We are social beings according to Fiske (2014). That means we have the ability to be sociable, to socialize, and to network with other human beings if we humans choose to do so. Most of the time contacts come from attending events, gatherings, social functions, or just being at the right place at the right time.

However, all these places that have been named will not help you to the fullest degree of what they can if you do not have the courage to go up to the people who are there at these events and talk to them or get them to talk. I too had to learn to be more social able. I was not always this way. As a matter of fact, I was shy and did not want to talk to people. I had to learn very slowly how to start up conversations. I have now become very good at doing so, probably to the point of mastery. I will share a little secret with you. One of the things that I discovered was what to say every time I shake someone's hand after I asked them their name, whether I was at a social event or not. This one question has led me to become more successful and develop greater business relationships that most of the time benefitted not only me, but also the person I was talking to. That question is, "What do you do?" This question alone has taken me to places that I would have never dreamed of going.

In many of my experiences, I have discovered that people generally do not mind sharing information, especially if you do not mind asking for it. You cannot expect people to come up to you and just give information as if they know or understand what's on your mind. If a person knows that he, or she needs information they have to go about obtaining it. One way to get great information that is directly related to a goal is to go to events, or places that encompass whatever it is you are pursuing. A good example for instance could be that there is a person that wants to write a book on art, and get real consumer input for his or her book. This person should go to an art gallery and strike up conversations with people who take artwork seriously. I learned that when striking up conversations with people to obtain information, it is best to let them talk. Some people may talk for a while, and the golden nugget may very well be at the end of what they are saying.

This is why it is important to let them finish and have pen and paper ready once the conversation is over to jot down critical data received. You would be surprised how much one can forget on the way to the next person. It has everything to do with details and remembering small critical amounts of information that will be exchanged between you and the other person (e.g., call me at this time, go to this place, search this website) and things of that nature. These little bits of information may very well be the golden keys to what you were looking for and the very things that would have catapulted you to another level of robust success! Therefore, do not make the mistake of losing them or letting them slip through the cracks.

There have been many cases when I will often ask a person to repeat something with pen and paper in my hand. You would be surprised how many people actually appreciate this method of receiving and retaining what they are saying because it shows them that what they are saying is important and appreciated by the listener. When I go to events that have something to do with one of my career choices, I look for people who are having group conversations. Once I pinpoint them, I go right up and stand there and listen. Sometimes it is good just to go up and listen and do not speak. Yes, wait to say hi later. You do not want to break up the flow of the conversation as this can be very awkward. Go up to the group conversation and show sincere interest.

Listen to what is being said, and if it does not fit what you are looking for, simply walk away. Believe me, they will not take it personally. Chances are they have the same method of operation and will know exactly what you are doing. If what they are saying piques your interest, stay there and listen attentively with your note pad and pen. When the conversation is over, introduce yourself and ask any necessary questions that you may have. These is welcomed most of the time, but keep it brief and ask for business cards because you can always call them later to request more critical information.

If the person is friendly and willing to share information on the spot, get all the information that you can. Only the inquiring minds will get the most valuable information. Always thank the person for the information you were provided with in a sincere way. From networking with a group of four to five people, I have discovered that those people will put me in contact with other people, and then contacts begin to multiply exponentially. I once heard Samuel L. Jackson say in an interview that every movie he does leads to his next film. So I came up with a method that could help and lead me to my next film. I would say casually to a producer or director, "What are you working on next?" This would most of the time get me in the door to be in my next film. It was a domino effect. It almost worked every time. The reason social gatherings occur is that so people can mingle and share information. This is how people acquire sources that have information. If and when one gets a source, they should work the source and not standby and do nothing. Meeting people will not destroy a person's career; it's not meeting important people that will.

Of course, a person wants to meet good solid people. Therefore, you will want to filter out the people who are not for you. I do this all the time, and it is nothing personal. Everyone you meet will not compliment your needs. You have to know how to distinguish for yourself, or you will simply waste your time. The same thing goes for when listening in on dynamic and non-dynamic group conversations. If the conversation is not for you, move on to the next conversation. Sometimes you will be listening, and the conversation may dramatically shift. This is your signal to move on to the next group conversation. Getting back to filtering out people, I clean my phone book out once a month. Moving forward, here are a few simple things you can do to increase your contacts in social functions and other important events.

The first thing you should do is have a business card drafted that tells what you do and give at least two ways that people can get in contact with you. Having a business card handy is impressive and shows people that you are serious about what you do. This will help you develop mostly serious contacts rapidly.

The second thing that you need to do is ask them for their business cards as well. If the person does not have a business card, write down their number or store it in your phone with an indicator that reminds you who they are, what they do, and where you met them at. Do this in a way that leaves them with a lasting positive impression. For instance, you may say something in the lines of "Don't worry about not having a card, sometimes I don't have mine, I can write it down." This shows them that you are not frowning on them for not having a business card, and they may have a greater chance of wanting to talk to you later. Never attend social functions and stand around as if you have a chip on your shoulder or looking as if you have an attitude problem.

When a person stands around, not talking to people, it can be construed that the person has an attitude or that they do not want to be approached by others. Looking and being approachable is very important to networking. Many people destroy their chances of gaining critical information because they appear as if they do not want to be bothered. Even if something is bothering you at a social function, it's probably best not to show it because it is highly likely that you will push people away.

When people go to social functions, they do not approach the person who looks as if they have a problem, so get out there, have your tools ready, and meet people. God made the world so that people, to some degree, are dependent upon other people. It is because of this fact that it pays to treat people with kindness and respect and learn to utilize social skills because without the proper social skills, people would not be as successful as they should be. With good social skills and networking power, a person has far more leverage to be where they want to be. It is, however, important to note that you cannot please everyone all the time.

However, you can do your best to treat people with respect and dignity, which will take you further than you ever imagined. People who have agoraphobia can seek psychological treatment plans to destroy the debilitating problem over the course of time. There are many ways to overcome anxiety caused by being around large crowds. Learning how to overcome your fears through therapy may very well be the one thing that will change your life for the better. Different types of therapy for those with agoraphobia include exposure therapy and cognitive-based therapy (CBT). Therapy may take time, but it is worth the investment for a better future!

*C*hapter 10

The Effect of The Magnetic Pull of The Sun in Our Solar System Manifested as Momentum in Human Beings

The Human Correlation Equation Factor

Momentum

New Trapped to Succeed Success Formula:

$$e + p = d^2 \text{ ™}$$

Energy plus momentum equals distance squared ©™

A new scientific equation created by

PhD candidate and author Eric Franklin Prince

I have called it *The Scientific Success Equation*©™

or the *Trapped to Succeed Success Formula*©™.

It is important that we as human beings understand that just as our sun has a magnetic pull on our earth, we as humans have things in our environment/atmosphere that have a magnetic pull on us. Whether they be negative or positive, there are elements within our universe that simply do. This is because we are a part of the cosmos and the universe that God created whether we like it or not. For we are, in all truth, organisms made up of energy that consist of various molecules, atoms, protons, electrons, and neutrons, along with other elements that derive from the universe. Some have termed these elements "stardust." This is why, all through this book, you have been observing pictures of the cosmos, which have been purposely and strategically placed in this book to spark a connection within you.

You may begin to subconsciously make a connection with the deepest aspects of yourself and your ability to make an effect in the world and throughout the universe! I want my readers to understand that if they can tap into and utilize their energy by finding what it is they love to do in life; this book may just very well provide them with great momentum, which will thrust them into exponential distances of success, where they will become trapped to succeed in life!

If one allows the energy of existing magnetic forces to influence them, they will be drawn toward that energy. Hopefully, that energy will be positive. The energy that is causing the magnetic pull on that person will contribute to that person gaining momentum toward that object or idea that will manifest as great distance and further success. This distance can be minuscule, or exponential in nature. It can be slow, or very rapid in pace, where it has the probability to continue on in nature without measure, which is why I squared the formula above (i.e., $e + p = d^2$). A good example that can be observed concerning success, or growth can be individuals who engage in advanced studies where they keep building and contributing to the growth and development of mankind, or one who continues to advance themselves continually throughout his or her life (i.e., obtaining a doctoral degree, or even being a hairstylist who never stops studying hair, learning how hairstyles evolve over time) with different types of cultures. Many different types of people can be represented here teachers, mechanics, cooks and so on.

Dr. Joel Paris alerts the scientific community and those becoming practitioners, as well as all others, to the fact that the brain is the most sophisticated organ in the entire known universe and that there are more synapses in the brain of a human being, than there are stars in our galaxy (Paris, 2015). This should alert humans to the very real fact that we are highly sophisticated, complex creatures with the ability for exponential growth. This is why human beings can become, without a doubt, trapped to succeed!

As a human being, you too can and will make ripple effects throughout the universe, just as other elements of matter and energy in the cosmos make gravitational waves throughout the universe according to Albert Einstein's gravitational wave theory. Human beings have the innate ability to do so with their thoughts and actions. As human beings, we are created in the image of God (Genesis 1:26, KJV). Therefore, we can release exponential amounts of positive gravitational waves throughout the universe that can and will manifest with major positive effects to our advantage for personal and shared success! I encourage you to make strong, positive gravitational waves in your life and in the lives of others, where you will become trapped to succeed!

For if gravitational waves are caused by coalescing neutron stars, according to the general theory of relativity discovered and documented by Einstein (1916) as cited by LIGO (2013), it is, therefore, my conclusion that because we are in part made up of neutrons and stardust, then other human beings, just as other successful people have done, can achieve great success.

This can and will happen if one will fuse their positive thoughts with powerful, positive actions, where these concepts will result in the exponential achievement of one's goals and dreams and where they will become locked into success and become trapped to succeed! This should be the goal during your lifetime, and I look forward to hearing great things from the readers of this book.

Eric F. Prince

FUTURE DIRECTIONS FOR PRACTITIONERS
WHO UTILIZE COGNITIVE-BASED
THERAPY TO ASSIST HUMAN BEINGS
IN BECOMING SUCCESSFUL

Expanding on Gordon Allport's concept of "nuclear quality," I would like to introduce a new concept that I have termed NQ-data, which takes the data of human dispositions (e.g., friendly, mean, happy, or sad) along with their unique goals, motives, and styles, and categorizes them into carefully thought-out charts. These charts can assist humans in understanding themselves by observing these concepts for higher levels of success in everyday life. It is very critical to understand that as humans, one's *disposition* will have an effect on their *unique goals* and that the *motives* of an individual can be positive or negative, which will also ultimately affect the outcome of one's goals. Last, the *style* and/or way of doing something can be extremely influential on how other human beings respond to members in societal settings. I propose that these concepts be charted and observed on a daily basis in therapeutic settings and for cognitive-based therapy homework assignments where clients may be able to come to the understanding that improving on these *nuclear qualities* can have the high probability of producing greater opportunities for exponential growth and development as it relates to higher rates of success in many areas of their lives.

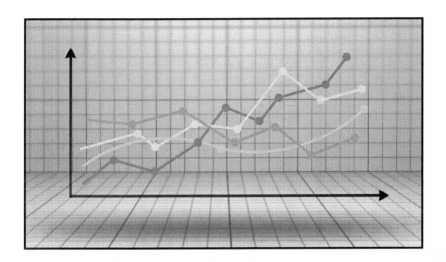

This chart can be adapted and repeated, where it displays the dispositions, *unique goals of the individual, the motives of the individual,* and the *style and/or way the individual* goes about doing things. If individuals can learn to chart themselves from one day to the next, they can improve on these nuclear qualities and learn to balance themselves over time, where their personal nuclear qualities become natural and instinctive. Humans can learn to consistently reach the higher percentages of the chart for improved quality of life.

A Brief Bonus: Chapter 11

Your Innate God-Given Resting Action Potential

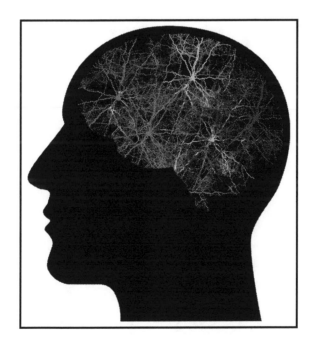

It is my belief that because of this innate quality that is hidden deep within us as humans, if we stretch out on our beliefs, even when they are difficult in nature or in scope or in sequence, our resting action potential will kick into gear and provide us with an extra boost of energy and oxygen to fulfill our goals. Some people may refer to this as a second wind. The question remains, however: Where did this second wind come from? I think I have discovered the answer, and I challenge scientists all over the world to confirm this thought.

The human makeup and/or the anatomical, biological, neurological, physiological, psychological, spiritual elements are very complex mechanisms. These processes have innate God-given biological, neurological, physiological resting action potentials that are deep within us and ready to be challenged to come out. It can be said that a person does not truly know what they are made of until they push themselves. I believe that this is when the resting action potential kicks in. As human beings, we really do not know what we can accomplish until we really and truly put forth the effort to discover what we can do.

We really do not know our fullest potential until we reach beyond that of our normal capability, which again is when the resting action potential kicks in on a higher level. This does not mean that it (the resting action potential) is not there for smaller tasks or for trivial physical-related responsibilities or things that we do on a daily basis.

I do, however, propose that the resting action potential is at rest because it can be at rest and is waiting for that moment when it is truly needed to respond to take action when we as humans reach a certain point and need the resting action potential to charge. It is important to understand that my hypothesis is predicated on the fact that the electrical potential of the inside of a cell is relative to its surroundings. Therefore, the resting action potential and the demand for the electrical charge potential will only be as great as it is needed to be because of the demand of the surrounding environment.

The next time you are seeking to complete a goal, and you are tired, worn out, and feel like stopping, remember your resting action potential. Remember that some goals take longer than others and that if you can keep your focus and maintain your pace of determination, you can and will get there, but it's up to you to block out interferences that come from internal and external stimuli or obstacles that come from inside you or outside of you. Becoming trapped to succeed is not an easy mission, especially when the goals are lengthy and require extreme amounts of discipline, but if you can really put your best foot forward, you will eventually reach your goal. This book has been designed for you to discover the arsenal of tools that are within you, that will inevitably cause you to become trapped to succeed.

A BRIEF EXPLANATION ON THE SCIENTIFIC SUCCESS FORMULA AND GOAL OF THE NEW LAW OF PHYSICS:

$E + P = D^2$:

ENERGY PLUS MOMENTUM
EQUALS DISTANCE SQUARED

After spending hours and hours going over the scientific success formula that I discovered for this book, which is for all, especially my readers, I further discovered that everything in the universe that is alive and that is achieving some form of goal must go through the law of physics and/or the scientific success formula ($e + p = d^2$).

Whether it is a spiritual entity or some other form of God's creation, such as human, terrestrial, or extraterrestrial, it is using this law of physics and/or success formula in some way to achieve its goals. It should be noted that although the formula seems simple in nature, there is much more to it than meets the eye.

For instance, an individual might not understand that to gain momentum, there must be a force that will either push or pull the energy forward. A good example could be a visual object that catches the eye. An entity with energy will observe an object and be attracted to the object because the object is a force to be reckoned with. The entity will gain momentum to go toward the object (distance), to interact with that object in some way, form, or fashion, and to gain some kind of result from it.

Example no. 1

A child full of energy will see candy (the force) in a candy store window and will be persuaded to come in its direction (the pull of momentum) and then go into the store (distance) to buy the candy and eat it, thereby having achieved success through the law of physics ($e + p = d^2$).

Example no. 2

A person possessing (energy) has a vision of building a house (force), he or she buys equipment and starts building the house (momentum), the house is finished 6 months later (distance) then the person moves into a fully functional house (success), because the goal is achieved.

Through these examples, an individual can see how that the law of physics and/or the success formula $e + p = d^2$ is being applied all over the world today. Whether we know it or not, we are using this formula. The goal of this book is to make the members of society aware of this formula, bringing it to their conscious minds.

Once we as humans understand this formula and that it can be applied consciously and systematically in our lives, there will be a greater probability to not allow internal or external forces to break the cycle of this law of physics and/or success formula in our lives. I could have written the success formula as $e + f + p = d^2$, but the force in this equation or in this law of physics is understood because an entity cannot gain momentum without the push or pull of a force. Therefore, I kept the formula that I originally created, which is e + p = d². *Force* is defined as a push or pull on an object that results from the object's interaction with another object (Meaning of Force, n.d). Whenever there is an interaction between two objects, there is a force upon each of the objects (Meaning of Force, n.d).

This scientific success formula, or should I say new law of physics and the application thereof, should assist societal members by causing them to understand what it means to stay the course and finish their goals. It is again my desire that this formula will be able to be utilized consciously and systematically in the pursuit of one's goals and dreams. It is my desire that when the world gets a hold of this success formula, they will use it in a positive way to become trapped to succeed in all that they do.

FUTURE ACADEMIC/NONFICTIONAL BOOKS FROM AUTHOR ERIC F. PRINCE

1. "Pre- and Post-Pregnancy Tips That Assist in Eliminating Stress and Postpartum Depression" ™

2. "The Unlock" ™

3. "Red Flags That Tell You When to Run from a Beginning Relationship" ™

4. "The Best Gift in Life: The Gift of Giving" ™

5. "What Is Love Really?" ™

6. "How to be Comfortable in Your Own Skin" ™

7. "The Beauty of Being Kind" ™

8. "Why Children Do What They Do: 'A Reflection of Piaget" ™

9. "The Critical Nature of Allowing Child Autonomy with Appropriate Oversight" ™

10. "Catching Happiness" ™

11. "Strategies for Maintaining Sound Mental Health" ™

12. "How to Become Trapped to Succeed: The Medical Doctor Blueprint Volume 3" ™

13. "How to Become Trapped to Succeed: The Lovely Truth about Marriage and How to Stay Happy Volume 4" ™

14. "How to Become Trapped to Succeed: A Revelation on Staying Blissfully Happy Volume 5" ™

15. "How to Become Trapped to Succeed: How to Use Flow to Maximize Living Life to the Fullest Volume 6" ™

16. "How to Become Trapped to Succeed: The Psychology of Time and Money Volume 7" ™

17. "How to Become Trapped to Succeed: How to Be Effective Godparents Volume 8" ™

FUTURE SPY THRILLERS BY WRITER/

ACTOR ERIQ F. PRINCE

The Agent Frank Crone Series

18. "Agent Frank Crone: The Rebirth of an American Spy" ™

19. "Agent Frank Crone: The Aftermath" ™

20. "Agent Frank Crone: Hump All Day-Hump All Night" ™

21. "Agent Frank Crone: From Chicago to LA" ™

22. "Agent Frank Crone: Situation: Damn Hot Mess" ™

23. "Agent Frank Crone: Operation: Clandestine Senator" ™

24. "Agent Frank Crone: Operation Covert Sky" ™

25. "Agent Frank Crone: If Looks Could Kill" ™

26. "Agent Frank Crone: The Beauty of It All" ™

27. "Agent Frank Crone: Operation Snow Blanket"

28. "Agent Frank Crone: The Monster behind the Mask" ™

29. "Agent Frank Crone: Operation: Rogue Shadow" ™

30. "Agent Frank Crone: Mission Snowfall" ™

31. "Agent Frank Crone: The Death of You" ™

32. "Agent Frank Crone: A Horrible Day to Die" ™

33. "Agent Frank Crone: No Rest till Sunrise" ™

34. "Agent Frank Crone: The Scantily-Clad Spy Killer" ™

35. "Agent Frank Crone: Operation Firestorm" ™

36. "Agent Frank Crone: Sick, Twisted, and Downright Ugly" ™

37. "Agent Frank Crone: Operation: Blackout" ™

38. "Agent Frank Crone: Situation: Beautiful Deadly Spy" ™

39. "Agent Frank Crone: Situation: Kill or Be Killed" ™

40. "Agent Frank Crone: Situation: Deranged Hyena" ™

41. "Agent Frank Crone: Situation: Invisible Tarantula" ™

42. "Agent Frank Crone: Situation: Tight Squeeze" ™

43. "Agent Frank Crone: Sexy Long-Legged Devil" ™

44. "Agent Frank Crone: No Rest until Nightfall" ™

45. "Agent Frank Crone: Project Choke Hold" ™

46. "Agent Frank Crone: No Dessert before Breakfast" ™

47. "Agent Frank Crone: Operation Iron Web" ™

48. "Agent Frank Crone: Operation Sundown" ™

49. "Agent Frank Crone: The Descension" ™

50. "Agent Frank Crone: Clean Slate - The Final Exam" ™

OTHER INSPIRING SELF-HELP BOOKS

1. *The 7 Habits of Highly Effective People* by Stephen R. Covey

2. *How to Stop Worrying and Start Living* by Dale Carnegie

3. *Rich Dad Poor Dad* by Robert T. Kiyosaki

4. *The Power of Now* by Eckhart Tolle

5. *You Can Heal Your Life* by Louise L. Hay

6. *How Successful People Think* by John C. Maxwell

7. *Think and Grow Rich!* by Napoleon Hill

8. *Discovering the Power of Positive Thinking* by Norman Vincent Peale

9. *The Alchemist* by Paulo Coelho

10. *What on Earth Am I Here For?* by Rick Warren

11. *High Performance Habits* by Brendon Burchard

12. The Law of Success by Napoleon Hill

OTHER RIVETING SPY THRILLERS

1. *The Bourne Identity*

2. *The Bourne Supremacy*

3. *The Bourne Ultimatum*

4. *The Bourne Legacy*

5. *Jason Bourne*

6. *Goldfinger* by Ian Fleming

7. *James Bond: Diamonds Are Forever*

8. *Mission Impossible*

9. *Kiss the Girls* by James Patterson

~ NOTES ~

The above seal is from Ghana, West Africa and represents vitality and renewal.

~ NOTES ~

The above seal is from Ghana, West Africa and represents vitality and renewal.

~ NOTES ~

_____

_____

_____

_____

_____

_____

_____

_____

_____

_____

_____

_____

_____

_____

_____

_____

_____

_____

_____

_____

_____

_____

_____

_____

_____

_____

_____

_____

_____

The above seal is from Ghana, West Africa and represents vitality and renewal.

~ NOTES ~

_____

_____

_____

_____

_____

_____

_____

_____

_____

_____

_____

_____

_____

_____

_____

_____

_____

_____

_____

_____

_____

_____

_____

_____

_____

_____

_____

_____

_____

_____

The above seal is from Ghana, West Africa and represents vitality and renewal.

~ NOTES ~

_____
_____
_____
_____
_____
_____
_____
_____
_____
_____
_____
_____
_____
_____
_____
_____
_____
_____
_____
_____
_____
_____
_____
_____
_____
_____
_____
_____
_____

The above seal is from Ghana, West Africa and represents vitality and renewal.

~ NOTES ~

The above seal is from Ghana, West Africa and represents vitality and renewal.

~ NOTES ~

_____

_____

_____

_____

_____

_____

_____

_____

_____

_____

_____

_____

_____

_____

_____

_____

_____

_____

_____

_____

_____

_____

_____

_____

_____

_____

_____

_____

_____

_____

_____

The above seal is from Ghana, West Africa and represents vitality and renewal.

~ NOTES ~

_____
_____
_____
_____
_____
_____
_____
_____
_____
_____
_____
_____
_____
_____
_____
_____
_____
_____
_____
_____
_____
_____
_____
_____
_____
_____
_____
_____
_____

The above seal is from Ghana, West Africa and represents vitality and renewal.

~ NOTES ~

The above seal is from Ghana, West Africa and represents vitality and renewal.

~ NOTES ~

_____

_____

_____

_____

_____

_____

_____

_____

_____

_____

_____

_____

_____

_____

_____

_____

_____

_____

_____

_____

_____

_____

_____

_____

_____

_____

_____

_____

_____

_____

The above seal is from Ghana, West Africa and represents vitality and renewal.

ABOUT THE AUTHOR

Photo by Marc Hauser Photography

Eric F. Prince has the strong desire to serve mankind by helping them achieve more abundant future in their lifetime. It is also Eric's desire to assist human beings by helping them learn to self-actualize, which is the innate process by which human beings learn to grow mentally, spiritually, and psychologically, where they will come into the realization of their fullest potential, which was and is the goal of Christ Himself (Friedman & Schustack, 2012; St. John 10:10, KJV).

Where there is no organization, there can be no creation.

References

American Psychiatric Association. (2013). *Diagnostic and Statistical Manual of Mental Disorders, 5th ed.* Arlington, VA: American Psychiatric Publishing.

American Psychological Association. (2015). *APA competency initiatives in professional psychology.* Retrieved from http://www.apa.org/ed/graduate/competency.aspx.

American Psychological Association. *(2010). Ethical principles of psychologists and code of conduct.* Retrieved from American Psychologist: http://apa.org/ethics/code/index.aspx.

American Board of Psychiatry and Neurology, Inc. (2007). ABPN Certification - Subspecialties. Retrieved from http://www.abpn.com/cert_subspecialties.htm.

Anderson, S., & Brownlie, J. (2011). Build it and they will come?

Understanding public views of "emotions talk" and the talking

therapies. British Journal of Guidance Ó Counselling, 59,

55-66. Retrieved from the Walden Library databases.

Annals of the American Psychotherapy/Association. (2010,

Summer). When clients can't afford therapy) Ways to help

them—and yourself-weather the nation's economic downturn,

13, 10. Retrieved from the Walden Library databases.

Berk, L. (2010). *Development through the Lifespan* (5th ed.). Allyn &

Bacon.

Bondi, M. W. (1992). Distinguishing psychological disorders from

neurological disorders: Taking Axis III seriously. *Professional

Psychology: Research and Practice, 23*(4), 306–309.

Brew, L., & Kottler, J. A. (2008). Applied helping skills:

Transforming lives. Thousand Oaks, CA: Sage.

Browne, S. (2004). Editorial. Counseling 6- Psychotherapy Journal,

15, 4-9. Retrieved from the Walden Library databases.

Bussolari, C. J., & Goodell, J. A. (2009). Chaos theory as a model for life transitions counseling: Nonlinear dynamics and life's changes. Journal of Counseling & Development, 87 (1), 98–107. Retrieved from the Walden Library databases.

Campbell, D. T. (1998). *Methodology and epistemology for social science:* Selected papers (E. S. Overman, ed.). Chicago: University of Chicago Press.

Carr, C. (2006, March 26). Mental health therapists face financial stress as fees stagnate. *New York Times*, p. 1. Retrieved from the Walden Library databases.

Colburn, A. A. Neuer. (2013). Endless possibilities: Diversifying service options in private practice. *Journal of Mental Health Counseling, Vol. 35* (3) pp. 198–210. Retrieved from the Walden Library databases.

Fiske, S. T. (2014). Social beings: Core motives in social psychology (2nd ed.). Hoboken, NJ: Awiley. Retrieved from the Walden University Databases.

Fouad, N. A., Grus, C. L., Hatcher, R. L., Kaslow, N. J., Hutchings, P. S., Madson, M. B.,... Crossman, R. E. (2009). Competency benchmarks: A model for understanding and measuring competence in professional psychology across training levels. *Training. Education in Professional Psychology, 3*(4, Suppl), S5–S26. Retrieved from the Walden Library databases.

Friedman, H. S., & Schustack, M. W. (2012). Personality: classic theories and modern research. (5th ed.). Allyn & Bacon.

Gomez-Pinella, F. (2008). Brain foods: the effects of nutrients on brain function. *Nature reviews neuroscience 9 (7)*, 568–578. doi:10.10 38/nrn2421.

Gomez-Pinella, F., & Tyagi, E. (2013). Diet and cognition: interplay between cell metabolism and neuronal plasticity. Retrieved from http://www.ncbi.nlm.nih.gov/pubmed/24071781. Current opinion in clinical nutrition metabolic Care. *16*(6):726-33. doi:10.1097/MCO.0b013e328 365aae3.

Hillman, M. (2006). A practice is born. Annals of the American Psychotherapy Association, 9, 41–42.

Ivey, A. E.; Ivey, M. B & Zalaquett, C. P. (2013). Intentional interviewing and counseling: Facilitating client development in a multicultural society. Cengage Textbook.

Johnson, M., O'Hara, R., Hirst, E., Weyman, A., Turner, J., Mason, S., ... Siriwardena, A. N. (2017). Multiple triangulation and collaborative research using qualitative methods to explore decision making in pre-hospital emergency care. *BMC Medical Research Methodology, 17* (1). doi:10.1186/s12874-017-0290-z.

Kaslow, N. J. (2004). Competencies in professional psychology.

American Psychologist, 59 (8), 774–781. Retrieved from the Walden Library databases.

Kaslow, N. J., Grus, C. L., Campbell, L. F., Fouad, N. A., Hatcher, R. L., & Rodolfa, E. R. (2009). Competency assessment toolkit for professional psychology. *Training and education in professional psychology, 3*(4, Suppl), S27–S45. Retrieved from the Walden Library databases.

Kiel, L. Douglas; Elliott, Euel W. (1997). Chaos theory in the social sciences. Perseus Publishing.

Krovetz, M. L. (2008). Fostering resilience: Expecting all students to use their minds and hearts well. *2ⁿᵈ ed,*. Thousand Oaks, California: Corwin Press.

Legge, D. (2012). Is private practice really for you? AMHCA Member Library: The business of private practice, Article 1. Retrieved from http://www.amhca.org/member/libraryl.aspx.

Lent, R. W. (2004). Toward a unifying theoretical and practical perspective on well-being and psychosocial adjustment. *Journal of Counseling Psychology, 51*(4), 482–509. Retrieved from the Walden Library databases.

Laser Interferometer Gravitational-Wave Observatory. (2013).

Retrieved from https://www.ligo.caltech.edu/page/what-are-gw.

Lomas, T. (2015). Positive Social Psychology: A multilevel inquiry into sociocultural well-being initiatives. *Psychology, Public Policy, and Law, Vol. 21*, No. 3, 338–347. Retrieved from the Walden Library databases http://dx.doi.org/10.1037/law0000051.

Jordan Michael. (2015). The Biography.com website. Retrieved fromhttp://www.biography.com /people/michael-jordan-9358066.

National Academy of Sciences. (2009). On being a scientist: A guide to responsible conduct in research/Committee on Science, Engineering, and Public Policy, National Academy of Science, National Academy of Engineering, and Institute of Medicine of the National Academies. — 3rd ed.

National Institute of Mental Health. (2015). Mental health medications overview. Retrieved from http://www.nimh.nih. gov/health/topics/ mental-health-medications/mental-health-medications.shtml.

NCSPP. (2007). Competency Developmental Achievement Levels (DALs) of the National Council of Schools and Programs in Professional Psychology (NCSPP). Retrieved from http://www.ncsp.

Oxford Reference. (n.d). Metacognition. Retrieved from http://www.Oxford reference.com/view/10.1093/oi/ authority.20110803100152784.

Oxford University Press. (2015). Oxford Dictionary Language Matters. Retrieved from http://www.oxforddictionaries.com/ definition/english/organization.

Paris, J. (2015). The intelligent clinician's guide to the DSM-5 (2nd ed.). New York, NY: Oxford University Press.

Seaford, C. (2014). What implications does well-being science have for economic policy? In T. J. Hämäläinen & J. Michaelson (eds.), Wellbeing and beyond: Broadening the public and policy discourse (pp. 221–243). Cheltenham, UK: Edward Elgar Publishing. Retrieved from the Walden Library databases.

The Meaning of Force. (n.d.). Retrieved from http://www.physics classroom. com/class/newtlaws/Lesson-2/The-Meaning-of-Force.

Tufan, A. E., Bilici, R., Usta, G., & Erdoğan, A. (2012). Mood disorder with mixed, psychotic features due to vitamin B12 deficiency in an adolescent: Case report. *Child And Adolescent Psychiatry And Mental Health*, 6doi:10.1186/1753-2000-6-25.

Vogiatzoglou, A., Refsum, H., Johnston, C., Smith, S. M., Bradley, K. M., de Jager, C., Budge, M. M., & Smith, A. D. (2008). Vitamin B12 status and rate of brain volume loss in community-dwelling elderly. Department of Physiology, Anatomy and Genetics, University of Oxford. Oxford UK. Retrieved from http:// limitlessmindset. com/scientific-studies/528-vitamin-b12-status-and-rate- of- brain-volume-loss.html#sthash.Sl1ZAN66.dpuf.

Wallace, S. L., Lee, J., & Lee S. M. (2010). Job stress, coping strategies, and burnout among abuse-specific counselors, journal of Employment Counseling, 47, U 1-122. Retrieved from the Walden Library databases.

Williams, E. N., Polster, D., Crizzard, M. B., Rockenbaugh, J., & Judge, A. B. (2003). What happens when therapists feel bored or anxious? A qualitative study of distracting self-awareness and therapists' management strategies, journal of Contemporary Psychotherapy, 33, 5–18. Retrieved from the Walden Library databases.

Printed in the United States
By Bookmasters